AUGUST'S

WORKBOOK TO ACCOMPANY

CNA:
NURSING ASSISTANT
CERTIFICATION

CALIFORNIA EDITION

SECOND EDITION

Lisa Rae Whitley, RN, ADN

AUGUST
LEARNING SOLUTIONS

Workbook to accompany CNA: Nursing Assistant Certification, California Edition,
Second Edition
Lisa Rae Whitley, RN, ADN

Copyright © 2025, August Learning Solutions

Published by August Learning Solutions
Cleveland, OH

August Learning Solutions concentrates instructor's efforts to create products that provide the best learning experience, streamlining your workload and delivering optimal value for the end user, the student.

www.augustlearningsolutions.com

Print ISBN: 978-1-941626-82-5
EPUB ISBN: 978-1-941626-67-2

29 28 27 26 25   10 9 8 7 6 5 4 3 2 1

Textbook activity answers, instructor resources, test bank questions, and workbook answer keys are available to instructors via the Instructor Portal.

Contents

Module 1: Introduction

1.A   Matching Definitions

_____ 1. Family Medical Leave Act (FMLA)

_____ 2. Health Insurance Portability and Accountability Act (HIPAA)

_____ 3. Delegated task

_____ 4. Informed consent

_____ 5. Occupational Safety and Health Administration (OSHA)

_____ 6. Ombudsman

_____ 7. Scope of practice

_____ 8. RCAC

_____ 9. CBRF

_____ 10. Respite care

_____ 11. Acute care facility

_____ 12. Responsibility

_____ 13. Chain of command

_____ 14. Mandatory reporter

_____ 15. Title 22

_____ 16. Assisted-living community

_____ 17. Rights

_____ 18. OBRA

_____ 19. Joint Commission

_____ 20. Hospice

_____ 21. Ethics

_____ 22. Long-term care facility

A. A facility that bridges the gap between living independently and living in a healthcare facility such as a nursing home

B. Someone who, as part of their job, must report any abusive or unlawful activity immediately

C. Offers care for residents needing skilled-nursing care for a substantial length of time

D. A volunteer who helps to protect the rights of residents by investigating complaints or reports of resident rights violations

E. Services that provide a safe and stimulating environment for older adults or developmentally disabled clients over the age of 18, normally during daytime hours

F. A facility that is comparable to senior apartment living and that offers minimal care

G. The California Code of Regulations that provides information about nurse aide training programs and other healthcare licensing regulations

H. An entity that accredits and surveys most acute care facilities in the United States

I. Legislation that mandated many regulations regarding the care of residents, resident rights, and the training requirements for nursing assistants

J. A hierarchical route of communication from one member of the healthcare team to the next

K. A job or action that a supervisor asks you to complete either verbally or through a written care plan

L. Entitlements; beliefs or laws that provide freedom to act in certain ways

M. The responsibilities, skills, and actions that you are permitted and expected to follow after you have completed your training

definitions continued on next page

N. A law that allows an employee to take a leave of absence from their job for a total of 12 weeks out of any 12-month period for certain medical needs without the risk of losing their job

O. Accountability for one's choices and actions

P. Offers specialty end-of-life care for residents who have less than 6 months to live

Q. A privacy law created in 1996 that protects all healthcare information that can be linked to an individual, known as individually identifiable health information

R. Legislation created in 1970 that ensures that all employees have safe and healthy working conditions

S. Principles of right and wrong that drive our behavior

T. The right to know what treatment options are available, and the risks associated with those treatments; the resident then has the right to make a choice about those options

U. One type of assisted-living community

V. A healthcare facility that provides short-term care for residents who have an immediate illness or injury

1.B   Reflective Short-Answer Exercises

Steve just started working in a nursing home. Their previous job was as a personal care worker at an assisted-living facility. Even though they are comfortable caring for residents, they find working at the new facility challenging and often confusing.

1. How are nursing homes and assisted-living facilities different from each other?

_____

_____

_____

_____

2. Why is Steve struggling in their new job at the nursing home?

_____

_____

_____

_____

3. How is taking care of the same type of resident different in various settings?

_____

_____

_____

_____

4. Do regulating bodies make a difference in the nursing assistant's job duties? If so, how?

_____

_____

_____

_____

5. What could Steve have done on their first day at the nursing home to make the transition easier?

_____

_____

_____

_____

1.C   Fill in the blanks using terms found in the word bank.

Omnibus Budget Reconciliation Act	dying	refuse
scope of practice	chain of command	document
nurse aide registry	provide personal care	home health aides
work ethic	acute care	respectful
reinforce	Medicare	hospice
home care	Continuing Care Retirement Community	advanced directives

1. Nursing homes are regulated by the _____.

2. _____ is often used in the military setting and also works well in healthcare.

3. The nursing assistant must _____ a task that is not within their scope of practice.

4. The goal of _____ is not to cure, but to assist the resident and family with the _____ process.

5. Part of your responsibility as the nursing assistant is to understand your _____.

6. Once a task is completed, the nursing assistant must _____ what was done.

7. _____ may be an option for a resident who needs healthcare services but chooses to remain in their own environment.

8. _____ is often used as payment for home health care, which is usually a temporary service.

9. You must be _____ of the alternative choices made by your resident.

10. A _____ combines independent living, assisted living, skilled nursing, and memory care all on one campus.

11. Living wills and _____ are legal documents that allow a resident to state who can make choices for them in the event they cannot make them for themselves.

12. One of the primary duties of a nursing assistant is to _____.

13. A(n) _____ facility is one that provides short-term care to patients who have an immediate illness or injury.

14. After the initial teaching is done by a nurse, the nursing assistant can _____ what has been taught to the resident.

15. The _____ is a database for employers to verify that you are a certified nursing assistant in good standing.

16. Part of acting professionally means you have a strong _____.

17. _____ may shop or run errands as well as provide daily caregiving.

1.D Multiple-Choice Exercises

1. You have noticed that one of your residents is more agitated and upset after starting a new medication. You should report this to the

   a) director of nursing.
   b) staff nurse.
   c) resident's healthcare provider.
   d) resident's husband.

2. The care plan for one of your residents states that they must have their back brace applied before they are to get out of bed in the morning. You are unsure how to do this, so you should

   a) ask one of your coworkers to apply the brace.
   b) have the resident tell you how they normally wear it.
   c) explain to the nurse that you do not understand the directives.
   d) have the nursing assistant from the previous shift apply it before they leave.

3. The most expensive type of healthcare setting is usually a(n)

   a) assisted-living community.
   b) hospice organization.
   c) respite care facility.
   d) acute care facility.

4. To ensure that hospitals are in compliance with federal regulations, they are surveyed by the

   a) Joint Commission at least every year.
   b) Joint Commission at least once every 3 years.
   c) Accreditation Commission for Healthcare every 6 months.
   d) Healthcare Quality Association every 2 years.

5. OBRA is federal legislation that regulates

   a) rehabilitation hospitals.
   b) long-term care facilities.
   c) respite care services.
   d) home health agencies.

6. A nursing assistant who works for a long-term care facility would most likely be caring for a resident who

   a) needs 24-hour care due to their dementia.
   b) had heart surgery 2 days ago.
   c) needs supervision and activities while their family is shopping.
   d) needs assistance only with medications and meals.

7. You are a new nursing assistant and work well in a fast-paced, changing environment. You might enjoy working

   a) on the medical-surgical floor at a local hospital.
   b) at a skilled nursing facility (SNF) with dementia care.
   c) at a chiropractic clinic assisting with exercises.
   d) for a home healthcare agency.

8. A nursing assistant working in an acute care facility is likely to work with

   a) public health department staff.
   b) radiologists and radiology technicians.
   c) physician assistants.
   d) all of the above.

9. Respite care offers services for residents who need

   a) rehabilitation and extensive therapy.
   b) a safe environment for short periods of time.
   c) end-of-life care.
   d) close monitoring of vital signs.

10. Scope of practice for a nursing assistant includes

    a) checking a resident's blood sugar level.
    b) giving residents their ordered medications.
    c) removing a urinary catheter.
    d) offering emotional support to a hospice resident.

11. Due to OSHA regulations, healthcare entities must provide their employees with

    a) family medical leave.
    b) inexpensive health insurance.
    c) free hepatitis B vaccines.
    d) chicken pox vaccines.

12. It is in the nursing assistant's scope of practice to

    a) educate a resident on a new diet.
    b) remind a resident to perform their leg exercises.
    c) show a resident how to put on their wrist brace for the first time.
    d) instruct a resident on how to take a new medication.

13. A task that is NOT in the scope of practice for a nursing assistant is

    a) delivering medications.
    b) providing dementia care.
    c) assisting with daily living activities.
    d) aiding with basic personal care tasks.

14. A nursing assistant becomes certified in the state of California after they

    a) obtain criminal clearance.
    b) complete 75 hours of classroom training.
    c) pass the certification exam.
    d) both a and c.

15. You have been assigned to an unfamiliar unit at your facility. Even though it is a new area, you ask for directives from the nurse and start your shift. This is an example of being

    a) prompt.
    b) flexible.
    c) empathetic.
    d) compassionate.

1.E Choose the best response to the following scenarios.

1. A resident you have been caring for in the nursing home tells you they are going home. They will be receiving care from a home health agency and are not sure what to expect. You should tell the resident

    a) that you need to get your supervisor, who will give them more information about what to expect from their home health provider.
    b) that nursing home care is much better than home health care.
    c) not to worry and that everything will be fine.
    d) you know other residents who have been very happy with home health services.

2. A resident in your facility is upset to hear that the medication the doctor has ordered is not the same medication that they had read about in a current magazine. The appropriate response for the nursing assistant would be to

    a) immediately tell the nurse of the resident's concerns.
    b) inform the facility's Director of Nurses.
    c) ask the resident to explain their concerns and then report this to the nurse.
    d) let the other nursing assistants know so they do not upset the resident.

3. Your neighbor is in need of skilled nursing care. Their daughter asks you to explain the difference between long-term care and home care. The best response would be

    a) that long-term care is most appropriate for a resident who requires ongoing treatment around the clock.
    b) that home care is available only to residents who have a lot of money.
    c) to tell the daughter it would be best if they could move in and care for their mother.
    d) to tell the daughter to call their mother's doctor.

4. Your resident has been recently diagnosed with a serious illness and has been searching the Internet for information. Your resident is upset and tells you the information gathered regarding their illness says that they will die. The best response would be to

    a) call their family to report their comments.
    b) inform their that they should only read medical websites.
    c) suggest they contact their healthcare provider to further discuss any concerns.
    d) help the resident search online for healthcare services.

5. During the sixth week of your new hospital job, you realize the fast pace and constant demands are too difficult. How should you speak with your supervisor regarding these concerns?

    a) Tell the supervisor that you prefer to be assigned only residents whom you feel comfortable caring for.
    b) Ask your supervisor to assign the other nursing assistants some of your tasks.
    c) Ask your supervisor if you can talk about other opportunities available in the facility that could be a better fit for your personality type.
    d) Tell your supervisor that you could do a better job if given more breaks during your shift.

6. The nurse you are working with asks you to perform a task that is not within your scope of practice. What is your best response?

    a) Tell the nurse that if they give you written instructions, you will perform the task.
    b) Politely remind the nurse that the task is not within your scope of practice.
    c) Inform the nurse that you are going to the director of nursing to report them for asking you to do something that is not within your scope of practice.
    d) Tell the nurse that you cannot perform the task, but you can find a nursing assistant who will.

7. Your resident in the assisted-living facility can no longer stand and needs more help than the staff can provide. The resident's daughter is very upset and asks you why their mother is being transferred to a long-term care facility. How should you answer them?

    a) Ask them to please wait while you get the supervisor, who can explain the situation in more detail.
    b) Inform them the facility is short staffed most of the time and cannot properly care for their mother.
    c) Tell them you're not sure, but whatever the reason their mother will be well cared for.
    d) Politely ask them not to ask you these types of questions because you do not make the decisions.

8. While caring for a resident in the nursing home where you work, a doctor enters the room and gives you instructions on how to properly care for the resident's heel wound. What is your best response?

    a) Listen carefully and report to the nurse the instructions given to you.
    b) Tell the doctor to please write the information down and that you will give that to the nurse when they return.
    c) Ask the doctor to wait while you get another nursing assistant to make sure you understand the instructions.
    d) Inform the doctor that you are the resident's nursing assistant but that you would be happy to find a nurse to assist them.

9. You are working the night shift at an assisted-living facility. Your coworker has been 20 minutes late every morning this week. You cannot leave until they get there. As a result, your kids have missed the bus. How would you resolve this situation?

    a) Inform the coworker that you will be reporting them to the supervisor.
    b) Remind the coworker that their shift starts promptly at 6:00 a.m. and explain why you cannot be late getting home.
    c) Talk to the other team members about how they are showing up late to work.
    d) Consistently show up 20 minutes late when you are relieving them from their shift.

10. Your home health resident asks you to explain the proper instructions given by the doctor regarding their recent hospital stay. What is your best response?

    a) Tell them that you are unable to give initial instructions but that you will call your supervisor.
    b) Instruct the resident to go online and find the proper information.
    c) Tell them that you will call the doctor and have them explain the instructions.
    d) Tell the resident that you will call their daughter and let them explain.

This page intentionally left blank.

Module 2: Patients' Rights

2.A Matching Definitions

_____ 1. Neglect

_____ 2. Abandonment

_____ 3. Negligence

_____ 4. Assault

_____ 5. Caregiver strain

_____ 6. Law

_____ 7. False imprisonment

_____ 8. Abuse

_____ 9. Misappropriation of funds

_____ 10. Battery

A. When caregivers emotionally can give no more to residents and start to treat residents or others poorly

B. A rule that you are legally obligated to follow

C. When care, treatment, or a service is not provided and the resident is then harmed

D. Threatening a resident with physical, mental, or emotional harm

E. When a caregiver does not follow the standards or scope of practice or the role that they are working in; they are not doing what a reasonable person would do in a given situation

F. When a caregiver walks away from their assignment before the end of the shift or before their replacement is there to relieve them, leaving residents alone and at risk

G. When a resident is limited from moving freely about their environment

H. Physically touching a resident when you do not have permission to do so

I. Intentionally using another person's money or belongings without that person's permission

J. A single or repeated action that is purposeful and meant to cause harm; can be mental, physical, sexual, or emotional

2.B Reflective Short-Answer Exercises

Judy is supposed to be transferred with a mechanical lift by two nursing assistants, as delegated by their care plan. This evening, one of the CNAs chose to transfer Judy by themself because it was quicker. Judy fell during the transfer. They were transferred to the emergency room to be evaluated, where it turned out that they suffered a broken hip.

1. Was the nursing assistant abiding by their responsibilities as an employee? Why or why not?

_____

_____

_____

_____

2. What would have been the ethical choice for the nursing assistant to have made in this scenario?

_____

_____

_____

_____

3. What was the negligent action in this scenario?

_____

_____

_____

_____

4. What do you think will happen to the nursing assistant in regard to employment?

_____

_____

_____

_____

2.C   Fill in the blanks with terms from the word bank.

caregiver strain	touching	abuse
knock	services	purposeful
treatment	survey	abuse
refuse	permission	isolation

1. State inspections of facilities use OBRA 1987 and state regulations to guide the _____ process.

2. Abuse is a single or repeated action that is _____ and meant to inflict harm.

3. Some caregivers turn into abusers due to _____.

4. Physically _____ a resident when you do not have permission is battery.

5. _____ can also be defined as repetitively withholding care.

6. Neglect occurs when _____ or _____ are not provided and the resident is harmed because of it.

7. _____ occurs when a resident is secluded from others against their wishes.

8. Touching a resident when you do not have _____ to do so is battery.

9. The nursing assistant should always _____ before entering a resident's room.

10. A resident has the right to _____ any treatment or action.

11. If the nursing assistant deliberately does not reposition a resident as scheduled, and the resident develops a bedsore, this is considered _____.

2.D Multiple-Choice Exercises

1. You are working as a nursing assistant at the local hospital when your replacement calls to say they will be late. You need to leave right away at the end of your shift. You should

    a) ask the nurse if they can call another nursing assistant to help.
    b) have the nurse work for you until your relief can get there.
    c) continue to work until your relief arrives.
    d) discuss the situation with the hospital administrator.

2. Juanita is a resident who has been using their call light frequently throughout your shift. You decide to ignore their call light since you have been in their room so often. Juanita attempts to reach their bathroom unassisted and falls. This is an example of

    a) abandonment.
    b) abuse.
    c) false imprisonment.
    d) neglect.

3. Jane is an older resident who is unable to move on their own. Their care plan states that they are to be repositioned every 2 hours. You have been especially busy, and you decide that you are able to reposition them only every 4 hours. Because of this, Jane develops a bedsore on their tailbone. This is an example of

    a) physical abuse.
    b) battery.
    c) neglect.
    d) both a and c.

4. Health and safety codes are the laws and regulations in the state of California that protect

    a) employers.
    b) residents.
    c) physicians.
    d) caregivers.

5. You suspect that one of the other nursing assistants has been verbally abusive to one of your residents. The best response would be to

    a) confront your coworker.
    b) report your suspicions to your supervisor.
    c) find out if your suspicions are correct and then report.
    d) tell the resident's family so they can keep the resident safe.

6. One of your coworkers is in the main doorway of your facility when you hear them talking about a resident who was especially challenging that day. The BEST response would be to

    a) join in the conversation to decrease your own stress.
    b) allow them to express their frustration.
    c) remind them that they should not talk about residents in a public area.
    d) immediately report the situation to the supervisor.

7. You are assisting a resident to the common dining room and lock their wheelchair brakes so they remain at the dining table until their meal arrives. This is an example of

    a) neglect.
    b) abandonment.
    c) false imprisonment.
    d) negligence.

8. Patient rights listed in the California Code of Regulations include all the following EXCEPT to

    a) be informed by a physician of their health status.
    b) consent to or refuse any treatment.
    c) have a phone in their room.
    d) have daily visiting hours established.

9. Using a resident's phone without their knowledge is an example of

    a) misappropriation of funds.
    b) caregiver strain.
    c) negligence.
    d) invasion of privacy.

10. According to California Title 22, the first eight hours of orientation for a nursing assistant recently hired at a long-term care facility will consist of

    a) emergency procedures.
    b) patient care policies.
    c) how to keep residents comfortable.
    d) nursing assistant training requirements.

2.E Choose the best response to the following scenarios.

1. Your resident appreciates the care you provide and offers you $20 as a tip. How should you respond?

    a) Gladly accept the tip for your good work.
    b) Thank the resident and tell them that you cannot accept tips.
    c) Tell the resident that you can accept only small tips.
    d) Split the $20 tip among your coworkers.

2. A resident asks you for a copy of their medical record. How would you respond?

    a) Tell the resident that they do not have the right to their personal records.
    b) Make copies of the medical record for the resident.
    c) Report your resident's request to the nurse.
    d) Read the medical record to the resident.

Module 3: Interpersonal Skills

3.A Matching Definitions

_____ 1. Projection

_____ 2. Empathy

_____ 3. Denial

_____ 4. Ethnicity

_____ 5. Therapeutic communication

_____ 6. Communication disorder

_____ 7. Defense mechanisms

_____ 8. Cultural competence

_____ 9. Nonverbal communication

_____ 10. Culture

_____ 11. Expressive aphasia

_____ 12. Repression

_____ 13. Autism

_____ 14. Verbal communication

_____ 15. Receptive aphasia

A. The national, cultural, or racial group that a person belongs to

B. To have understanding and compassion for others

C. When the subconscious brain ignores thoughts or situations to protect oneself

D. A way to protect one's self when feeling anxious or upset; may include denial, repression, or projection

E. A way of combining active listening skills and acknowledging feelings

F. A speech or language problem that results in impaired interactions with others

G. When one can accept the differences between one's self and the resident; willingly incorporating the resident's belief system into the caregiving process

H. Expressing information or ideas through the use of speech

I. Refusing to experience or accept a situation

J. A neurological disorder that impairs communication and social interaction

K. The use of body language and facial expressions to convey ideas or emotions

L. The inability to speak or to speak clearly

M. The inability to understand spoken language

N. A set of traditions and attitudes that are shared within a group of people

O. Attributing feelings or thoughts to another person

3.B Reflective Short-Answer Exercises

Carter is a 49-year-old resident with autism. They have expressive aphasia, with limited speech ability. They have not bonded with any of the staff at the long-term care facility where they live. They become frustrated with the staff when a staff member does not understand what they are trying to say. You are taking care of Carter this evening and need to help them get ready for bed.

1. Do you think Carter has a communication disorder?

    _____

    _____

    _____

    _____

2. How could you help Carter in regard to their expressive aphasia?

    _____

    _____

    _____

    _____

3. Does Carter have a neurological or communication disorder? Or both?

    _____

    _____

    _____

    _____

4. What interventions can you use to assist Carter in regard to their autism?

    _____

    _____

    _____

    _____

3.C   Fill in the blanks using terms found in the word bank.

acquired	hearing loss	responsibility
stress	active listening	culture
training	language	verbal
aphasia	challenging	social awareness

1. "You" statements place _____ on the other person and can make the situation more _____ .

2. Residents may suffer from expressive or receptive _____, which means that either the resident is unable to speak or to speak clearly, or the resident is unable to understand spoken language.

3. It is important to consider the resident's _____ and ethnicity when providing care.

4. When speaking with a resident who has _____, make sure that they can see your face.

5. A communication disorder is a speech or _____ problem that results in impaired interactions with others.

6. The best way to communicate your expectations to the resident is by using _____ communication.

7. The nursing assistant should always request _____ on new equipment before assisting the resident.

8. Using the right communication techniques in healthcare can help reduce _____ and help the resident feel more comfortable.

9. Truly hearing what the person talking to you is saying is _____.

10. Using the correct pronouns when addressing a resident or colleague is an example of _____.

11. Communication disorders can be either congenital or _____.

3.D   Multiple-Choice Exercises

1. Melissa is a resident with severe hearing loss. They have an assistive listening device that they use with their hearing aid. You are not sure how to use their listening device. You should

   a) ask Melissa how to use the device and hearing aids.
   b) get another nursing assistant to help you with Melissa's care.
   c) request training on the listening device before helping Melissa.
   d) ask Melissa's family to show you how to use the device.

2. Emotional communication deficits can be a result of

   a) stroke.
   b) post-traumatic stress disorder.
   c) hearing loss.
   d) expressive aphasia.

3. Judah has a hearing deficit from working in construction for many years. This is an example of

   a) a congenital hearing loss.
   b) an acquired hearing loss.
   c) a neurological disorder.
   d) expressive aphasia.

4. Mr. Lee is a new resident at your facility. Their family has just left, and you notice that they are upset and teary. When you enter their room, they say they want to go home. You should

   a) tell them that this is the best facility their family could have put them in.
   b) assure them that the staff is very kind and helpful.
   c) sit quietly with them and let them talk when they are ready.
   d) leave the room to give them privacy.

5. When caring for a resident with expressive aphasia, you should

   a) speak slowly and clearly.
   b) use short, direct sentences.
   c) use a picture board or book.
   d) talk in a normal pitch of voice.

6. When communicating with a resident who has hearing loss, you should do all of the following EXCEPT

   a) raise the pitch of your voice.
   b) speak at eye level with the resident.
   c) slow your speech down.
   d) use a picture board.

7. You are caring for a resident who comes from a different background than you do. You do not agree with the resident's beliefs and lifestyle. How should you care for this resident?

   a) Try to convince the resident that they are wrong and you are right.
   b) Care for the resident without regard to background or lifestyle while putting your personal opinions aside.
   c) Ask the nurse to instruct the resident to change their ways.
   d) Ask a coworker to care for the resident to avoid conflict.

8. Virgil is a resident recovering from a recent stroke. They often become frustrated because they are not able to understand your directives. This is an example of

   a) receptive aphasia.
   b) expressive aphasia.
   c) congenital hearing loss.
   d) an emotional deficit.

9. When caring for a resident with vision impairment, you can do which of the following to be respectful and maintain resident safety?

   a) Change placement of furniture and objects in the room
   b) Use a clock face to describe where items are located
   c) Use good lighting
   d) Both B and C

10. You are caring for a resident when their daughter arrives to visit. While visiting, the daughter becomes upset and starts yelling at the resident. You believe the situation will become physically abusive. The BEST response is to

    a) contact the authorities.
    b) tell the daughter they are no longer allowed to visit.
    c) leave the room and return when the daughter is calmer.
    d) provide the resident and their daughter time to speak privately.

3.E Choose the best response to the following scenarios.

1. You are having trouble communicating with your hearing-impaired resident, and they are becoming upset and frustrated. What is the BEST response?

   a) Refer to their care plan to identify any communication techniques that will help you.
   b) Try sign language; you learned this in high school.
   c) Raise the pitch of your voice so they can hear you.
   d) Return to the resident later when they are no longer angry.

2. While you are assisting a resident with their shower, they become angry and start hitting you on the face and arms. What should you do FIRST?

   a) Back away from the resident and allow them time to calm themself.
   b) Use active listening techniques to determine why they are upset.
   c) Assist them out of the shower so they will not fall and injure themself.
   d) Report the incident to your supervisor.

3. Carla is a resident with receptive aphasia. They often become upset when they don't understand your directives during care. How can you best care for them?

   a) Ask the resident to speak slowly and clearly.
   b) Break tasks up into smaller steps.
   c) Write your directives on a whiteboard.
   d) Ask for an interpreter.

Name _____

4. You enter your resident's room and find them grimacing and holding their stomach. The best response is to

   a) assist them to the bathroom.
   b) ask them if they are OK and be prepared to assist if needed.
   c) tell the nurse they are in pain and need medication.
   d) come back later when they are feeling better.

This page intentionally left blank.

Module 4: Prevention and Management of Catastrophe and Unusual Occurrences

4.A Matching Definitions

_____ 1. Employee assistance plan (EAP)

_____ 2. RACE

_____ 3. Safety Data Sheets (SDSs)

_____ 4. PASS

A. OSHA-mandated sheets that give detailed information about what each chemical is and what first aid to use if an exposure occurs; they also list information on how to use the chemical, how to store or dispose of it, and what protective equipment is needed with use

B. An agreement between the employer and an insurance company and/or a mental health provider to provide employees with free mental healthcare services for themselves or a family member

C. Acronym used to remember how to respond to a fire

D. Acronym used to remember how to use the fire extinguisher

4.B Reflective Short-Answer Exercises

Herman is an older person with dementia. They are no longer safe to stay at home alone because they have been wandering out of their home and getting lost. Home health care is not an option, since they need 24-hour supervision. Herman's daughter is trying to decide which long-term care facility is best for Herman.

1. What minimum requirements should Herman's daughter expect at each long-term care facility in regard to the physical environment?

_____

_____

_____

_____

2. What should Herman's daughter be looking for when touring the individual rooms at each long-term care facility?

_____

_____

_____

_____

3. Are there certain indicators of cleanliness and safety that the daughter should be looking for while touring the facilities?

_____

_____

_____

_____

4. What factors would indicate poor quality of care?

_____

_____

_____

_____

5. What should each facility look like?

_____

_____

_____

_____

6. What should each facility smell like? What steps can staff take to prevent the facility from smelling?

_____

_____

_____

_____

4.C   Fill in the blanks with terms found in the word bank.

employer	dining	OSHA
chemical	workplace violence	rights
water	call-light system	dangerous
bathroom	privacy	safety
activities	insurance company	blood-borne pathogens
emergency plans	alarm systems	needlestick injury

1. _____ are tools occasionally used to alert staff that at-risk residents may be in danger.

2. An agreement between the _____ and a(n) _____ may provide employees with free mental healthcare services for themselves or a family member via an EAP.

3. Employers are mandated by _____ to offer the hepatitis B vaccine series to all workers who may be exposed to blood-borne pathogens.

4. _____ can be found in body fluids other than blood, such as vomit, saliva, urine, feces, semen, vaginal secretions, and wound drainage.

5. _____ is a basic human right and need.

6. There must be a minimum of one common room for _____ and _____ in each long-term care facility.

7. Working in healthcare can be _____ if you do not follow your employer's and OSHA's policies.

8. Every healthcare facility must have _____ in place in the event of a natural disaster.

9. In 1987, Congress mandated that residents in long-term care (LTC) facilities have certain _____.

10. The Omnibus Budget Reconciliation Act (OBRA) includes resident rights such as safety, respect, _____, and quality of life.

11. The long-term care facility must guarantee a safe _____ supply.

12. In older long-term care buildings, there may not be a(n) _____ within each resident room, so residents might have to share.

13. _____ is much more common in healthcare than in other types of employment.

14. A(n) _____ must be in place and operational to ensure the safety of long-term care residents.

15. In the event of a _____ you should obtain HIV and hepatitis tests as well as fill out an incident report after obtaining medical help.

16. Safety Data Sheets (SDSs) give detailed information about what each _____ is and suggest what first aid to use if an exposure occurs.

4.D   Multiple-Choice Exercises

1. Information found in the SDS includes

    a) the resident's diagnosis and care plan.
    b) how to store or dispose of chemicals.
    c) ergonomic recommendations.
    d) fire safety plans.

2. You have just entered the dining area when you notice smoke coming from the kitchen. Your FIRST response should be to

    a) call the fire department.
    b) pull the fire alarm.
    c) grab the fire extinguisher.
    d) place residents beyond the fire doors.

3. Healthcare workers are at risk of exposure to blood-borne pathogens present in

    a) urine and feces.
    b) wound drainage.
    c) vomit and saliva.
    d) all of the above.

4. When using a fire extinguisher, you should aim

    a) and sweep along the base of the fire.
    b) the extinguisher at the base and hold still.
    c) and sweep at the fire's flames.
    d) at the flames and hold still.

5. An employee assistance plan (EAP) is an agreement that provides

    a) free services to employees only.
    b) free services to employees and their families.
    c) health benefits to employers.
    d) health information to employers.

6. The call light in one resident's room is not working. The FIRST step you should take is to

    a) find a bell for the resident to use in place of the call light.
    b) ask the resident to sit at the nurses' desk.
    c) report the broken call light to the nurse.
    d) ask the facility's maintenance staff to fix the call light.

7. The MOST important step in protecting yourself from workplace violence is to

   a) keep doors locked at all times.
   b) work only with people you know and trust.
   c) watch for potentially dangerous situations.
   d) work during daytime hours.

8. In the case of an evacuation, the nursing assistant may have to

   a) go with the residents during transportation to a new area.
   b) take on laundry and kitchen duties.
   c) care for more residents than usual.
   d) do all of the above.

9. OBRA regulations apply to aspects of a resident's room and environment in

   a) acute care facilities.
   b) assisted-living centers.
   c) skilled nursing facilities.
   d) respite care facilities.

10. Long-term care facilities are required to have all of the following EXCEPT

    a) an air-conditioning system.
    b) hand rails on both sides of hallways.
    c) a fully equipped room for dining and activities.
    d) a safe water supply.

11. A pleasant homelike environment in a healthcare facility can improve

    a) resident comfort.
    b) consumer use of the facility.
    c) customer satisfaction.
    d) all of the above.

12. If a nursing home has a dining room too small for its residents and their equipment, the facility should

    a) leave the equipment outside the dining room.
    b) have some residents eat in their rooms.
    c) set up tables in the hallway.
    d) rotate the residents' meal times.

13. Maria is one of the residents you care for at a long-term care facility. Maria tells you that they have not been able to sleep because their roommate has a lot of family who visit in the evening. You should

    a) ask the family if they can visit in the common room.
    b) move Maria's roommate to a new room.
    c) move Maria to a new room.
    d) tell the family to visit during the day instead.

14. A nursing home that does not have fire evacuation plans in place is likely to

    a) lose its license to provide care.
    b) be cited and pay severe penalties.
    c) be unable to accept new residents.
    d) close until plans are made.

15. Sarah and their roommate have very different personalities and have not been getting along. Sarah is asking to move to a new room. You should

    a) move Sarah to a new room when it's available.
    b) explain that this is not an option for them.
    c) do nothing; this is not uncommon in long-term care.
    d) report their request to the nurse.

16. Resident bathrooms in a long-term care facility must be

    a) in each resident room.
    b) shared by no more than two residents.
    c) accessible to all residents.
    d) equipped with a tub and a shower.

4.E Choose the best response to the following scenarios.

1. While at work in the nursing home, you notice your hands start to itch; by the end of the day, you have a rash on your hands. What should you do?

   a) Wash your hands and report to your supervisor immediately.
   b) Use hand sanitizer instead of soap and water.
   c) Wear gloves to further eliminate any exposure.
   d) Update your supervisor if the rash doesn't go away after a few days.

2. You have noticed that one of your coworkers has come to work tearful and upset on several occasions. When you speak with them, they state, "Things aren't good at home." What should you do?

   a) Report your coworker's statements to the director of nursing.
   b) Contact authorities since this might indicate an abusive situation.
   c) Refer your coworker to the Employee Assistance Plan.
   d) Ask your coworker for more information before deciding what action to take.

3. You are working the night shift and notice many of your coworkers are talking and laughing very loudly. What should you do?

   a) Remind them that the residents are asleep.
   b) Join in if no residents have complained.
   c) Call the supervisor and report your coworkers' actions.
   d) Make sure all of the residents' doors are shut.

4. You are working as a nursing assistant in the nursing home, and you have a fire drill at the same time that you are scheduled to take your break. What should you do?

   a) Take your break as scheduled.
   b) Ask your coworkers what they would do.
   c) Request that the drill time be changed.
   d) Report to your supervisor for instruction.

5. While plugging in a resident's television, you notice a spark and smoke. What should you do?

   a) Wait and make sure the television works well.
   b) Tell the resident that they need to get it fixed soon.
   c) Unplug the television and report to the supervisor immediately.
   d) Bring in your television for the resident to use.

6. Your resident uses the call-light system every 10 minutes and you are getting frustrated. What should you do?

   a) Tell the resident to only use the call light in an emergency.
   b) Continue to answer the call light every time it is on.
   c) Ask your supervisor to move the resident to a closer room.
   d) Call the resident's family and ask them to visit the resident.

7. Two residents share a room. One resident is eating breakfast in the room, and their roommate is asking to use the bedside commode. What would you do?

   a) Pull the privacy curtain and place the resident on the commode.
   b) Explain that the roommate is eating and take the resident to a restroom.
   c) Tell the resident that they need to wait until the roommate is finished with breakfast.
   d) Cover the breakfast tray while the commode is being used.

8. While toileting a resident, you are accidentally exposed to urine. You wash the area thoroughly with soap and water. The NEXT step should be to

   a) have blood drawn for an HIV test.
   b) report the incident to your supervisor.
   c) fill out an incident report.
   d) obtain a medical evaluation.

9. While caring for a resident in their room, you hear the facility's fire alarm. The FIRST step you should take is to

    a) report to the nurse for directives.
    b) remove residents from the area of the fire.
    c) locate a fire extinguisher and extinguish the fire.
    d) evacuate residents from the facility.

Module 5: Body Mechanics

5.A Matching Definitions

_____ 1. Gait belt

_____ 2. Ergonomics

_____ 3. Trapeze

A. Adapting work style and the work environment to be safer; how a person safely moves about the environment and physically completes tasks while at work

B. An implement that attaches to the bed frame, extending out overhead and used for leverage by the resident for repositioning in bed

C. A device placed around the resident's waist for use when transferring and ambulating

5.B Reflective Short-Answer Exercises

Yvonne is a bariatric resident who prefers to remain in bed for much of the day. The nurse has directed you to assist Yvonne out of bed during meal times. Their care plan states that they need to be transferred with a two-person assist, a gait belt, and a walker.

1. You must reposition Yvonne in bed every 2 hours throughout your shift. What supplies could you use to assist with moving Yvonne up in bed?

_____

_____

_____

_____

2. What interventions could you use to assist them with sitting on the side of the bed, without physically lifting them up?

_____

_____

_____

_____

3. If Yvonne was not feeling well or could not follow your directives to stand, how could you safely transfer them into their wheelchair for breakfast?

_____

_____

_____

_____

5.C Fill in the blanks using terms found in the word bank.

safety	tripod	sleeping
waist	flat	bed frame
Fowler's	transferring	Sims's
repositioned	muscles	shearing
semi-Fowler's	prone	side-lying

1. A trapeze is an implement that attaches to the _____ and is used for leverage by the resident to reposition in bed.

2. Keep your feet apart, with a wide base of support and knees bent, when _____ residents.

3. Residents must be _____ every 2 hours while in bed and every 1 hour while in a wheelchair.

4. The nursing assistant assumes a wide stance and uses the large _____ of the hips, thighs, and buttocks during the resident movement to prevent injury to themself.

5. The head of the bed must be _____ before moving the resident up in the bed.

6. _____ is a form of side-lying position used when a resident needs an enema.

7. Placing shoes or nonskid slippers on a resident's feet during resident transfers is a very important _____ consideration.

8. The supine position is a comfortable _____ position for most people.

9. The head of the bed is raised to about 35–40 degrees in the _____ position.

10. _____ across the bed linens during repositioning should be limited as much as possible.

11. When in a _____ position, the resident should be positioned on the fatty part of their buttock.

12. Often, residents who suffer from respiratory disorders assume a _____ position.

13. A gait belt is a device placed around the resident's _____ during transferring and ambulating to keep the resident safe.

14. A resident in the _____ position is lying on their stomach.

15. The head of the bed is raised to anywhere between 45 and 60 degrees for the _____ position.

5.D Multiple-Choice Exercises

1. The position used for a resident who will be receiving an enema is

    a) Sims's.
    b) supine.
    c) semi-Fowler's.
    d) prone.

2. When a resident is in Fowler's position, pillows should be placed

    a) under the head and lower legs.
    b) under the head and shoulders.
    c) under the head only.
    d) behind the knees.

3. The position that puts a resident at greatest risk of shearing injuries to the back, sacrum, and coccyx is

   a) supine.
   b) high-Fowler's.
   c) side-lying.
   d) semi-Fowler's.

4. Positioning a resident properly in a wheelchair helps to

   a) prevent pressure injuries.
   b) decrease discomfort.
   c) reduce the risk of sliding out of the wheelchair.
   d) do all of the above.

5. You are transporting a resident in their wheelchair. Their feet drag on the floor because they are unable to keep their feet lifted while you are moving. You should

   a) place a cushion under their buttocks to keep their feet from touching the floor.
   b) place leg rests on the wheelchair if indicated on the resident's care plan.
   c) have a coworker hold their legs up while you transport the resident.
   d) pull the wheelchair backward so their feet do not get hurt.

6. One nursing assistant can move a resident up in bed if

   a) the resident has no side rails on their bed.
   b) the resident has a trapeze secured to the bed.
   c) the resident grabs the nursing assistant's arms for support.
   d) none of the above; repositioning requires a two assist.

7. When two nursing assistants move a resident up in bed, they should grasp the draw sheet

   a) 4 inches away from the resident's body.
   b) 6 inches away from the resident's body.
   c) as close to the resident's body as possible.
   d) as far from the resident's body as possible.

8. The most comfortable position for a resident with breathing problems is

   a) prone.
   b) supine.
   c) Sims's.
   d) Fowler's.

9. For repositioning a bariatric resident while in bed, you need to

   a) ask for help from at least one other coworker.
   b) use a top sheet, bath blanket, or bed blanket.
   c) ask the resident to help as much as they are able.
   d) do all of the above.

10. The nurse requests that you assist a resident into a tripod position. This is likely because they

   a) have difficulty breathing.
   b) will be getting an enema.
   c) are watching television while in bed.
   d) have a pressure injury on their coccyx.

11. Sarah is a resident who uses their wheelchair to move throughout the facility. They have leg rests on their wheelchair to keep their legs elevated. You help them to their room since they are unable to propel themself. Before leaving Sarah's room, you should

   a) remove the leg rests and hand them the call light.
   b) move the leg rests out to the side of their chair so they can keep their feet on the floor.
   c) position the leg rests according to the care plan and hand them the call light.
   d) do none of the above.

12. The FIRST step in transferring a resident from bed to wheelchair is to

   a) place the wheelchair at the foot of the bed.
   b) remove the leg rests from the wheelchair.
   c) tell the resident what you need them to do.
   d) check the resident's care plan for level of assistance needed.

13. To place a resident in a semi-Fowler's position, the head of the bed should be

    a) left flat.
    b) raised 35–40 degrees.
    c) raised 45–60 degrees.
    d) raised 80–90 degrees.

14. Before you assist a resident to stand, they must be wearing

    a) shoes or have bare feet.
    b) socks or bathroom slippers.
    c) footwear with a nonskid sole.
    d) what they find most comfortable.

15. Wearing shoes that are comfortable and have good arch support helps prevent injury to the nursing assistant by

    a) reducing the risk of trips and falls.
    b) reducing back strain.
    c) maintaining the back in good alignment.
    d) all of the above.

5.E Choose the best response to the following scenarios.

1. While ambulating your resident, they fall. You lower them safely to the ground using the gait belt they were wearing. The resident says they feel fine and are not hurt. What should you do?

    a) Help them stand and continue to ambulate since they are unhurt.
    b) Ask a coworker for assistance to continue ambulating.
    c) Update the supervisor before moving the resident.
    d) Get the mechanical lift and lift them to a chair.

2. Your resident refuses to allow you to use the gait belt as the care plan states. What should you do?

    a) Respect your resident's wishes and do not use the gait belt.
    b) Ask another nursing assistant to complete the transfer.
    c) Reinforce to the resident the importance of using the gait belt and report to the supervisor.
    d) Call the resident's family and inform them that the resident is refusing to use the gait belt.

3. Your resident is doing well and seems to be able to transfer with an assist of two nursing assistants and a gait belt instead of the mechanical lift as the care plan states. What should you do?

    a) Transfer the resident with two nursing assistants so they regain strength.
    b) Use the mechanical lift and report your findings to the supervisor.
    c) Transfer the resident with two nursing assistants and the gait belt for added safety.
    d) Ask your coworkers how they transferred the resident earlier in the day.

4. You are asked to boost a bariatric resident up in bed. The resident is unable to reposition themself but does have a trapeze attached to the bed frame. What should you do?

    a) Obtain enough assistance from staff to ensure that you do not injure your back.
    b) Do your best to boost the bariatric resident by yourself; they also have a trapeze to assist.
    c) Tell the resident that you are unable to perform this task.
    d) Use a mechanical lift to move the resident upward in bed.

5. Your resident has asked you to help them to the toilet. While you are trying to put your gait belt around the resident for this transfer, they say, "I need to go now!" They wave you away and try to stand up alone. What should you do?

    a) Let them stand up and ambulate without the gait belt.
    b) Stand in front of them while applying the gait belt and remind them of safety.
    c) Refuse to help them because they are at risk of injury.
    d) Tell them to wait in the bathroom while you get the nurse.

6. Your resident's care plan states to use a sit-to-stand device for transfers. You are not sure how to operate the sit-to-stand model being used for the resident. What should you do?

    a) Use an assist of two, gait belt, and walker for the transfer.
    b) Ask your supervisor for instruction.
    c) Read the instructions on the sit-to-stand device before use.
    d) Ask the physical therapist to transfer the resident.

7. John is a resident who has asked for assistance getting into their wheelchair. Their care plan states that they transfer with an assist of one and a gait belt. John has a colostomy that prevents you from placing the gait belt around their waist. What should you do?

    a) Place the gait belt above the colostomy.
    b) Use a mechanical lift for the transfer.
    c) Transfer them by lifting under their arms instead of using the gait belt.
    d) Empty the colostomy first, then place the gait belt across it.

8. Your resident has had several falls in the past. They are now refusing to ambulate because they are frightened that they might fall again. What should you do?

    a) Do not ambulate the resident if they are afraid.
    b) Tell them that it is required for good health.
    c) Provide encouragement to walk small amounts at a time.
    d) Call the resident's family and ask if they can convince the resident to walk with you.

This page intentionally left blank.

Module 6: Medical and Surgical Asepsis

6.A Matching Definitions

_____ 1. Germ

_____ 2. Contingency capacity

_____ 3. Conventional capacity

_____ 4. Personal protective equipment (PPE)

_____ 5. Immunity

_____ 6. Crisis capacity

_____ 7. Infection control

_____ 8. Primary prevention

_____ 9. Antibody

_____ 10. Germ theory

A. A microorganism that can be either a bacteria, virus, fungus, or protozoa

B. Preventing disease before it starts

C. Measures consisting of engineering, administrative, and personal protective equipment (PPE) controls that should already be implemented in general infection prevention and control plans in healthcare settings

D. Preventing or limiting the spread of germs

E. A body defense against a specific invader; produced by either a vaccine or exposure to the disease itself

F. Bodily defenses (antibodies) that prevent illness from occurring upon exposure to a specific germ

G. The idea that microorganisms are the cause of most illnesses

H. Specialty equipment that acts as a barrier between the healthcare worker and potentially infectious bodily fluid

I. Measures that may be used temporarily during periods of expected shortages

J. Strategies that are not commensurate with U.S. standards of care but may need to be considered during periods of known shortages

6.B Reflective Short-Answer Exercises

Jordan is an 80-year-old resident with pneumonia. They have been receiving antibiotics for the last 7 days. They seemed to be getting better, but today they have a fever. Jordan tells you their stomach does not feel well and that they have had explosive diarrhea all morning. You report this to the nurse promptly. The nurse places Jordan on contact precautions with strict hand washing. Later that day, it is confirmed that Jordan has a C. Diff infection.

1. If it were not for the work of Semmelweis and Pasteur, what might happen to Jordan?

_____

_____

_____

_____

2. What might happen to the healthcare workers taking care of Jordan?

_____

_____

_____

_____

3. What might happen to the other residents the healthcare workers are taking care of after helping Jordan?

_____

_____

_____

_____

4. What primary prevention action could have positively affected Jordan's hospital stay?

_____

_____

_____

5. What PPE would you use while toileting Jordan?

_____

_____

_____

_____

6. It was confirmed that Jordan has a C. Diff infection. Why do you think Jordan became infected with C. Diff?

_____

_____

_____

_____

7. Is it appropriate to hand sanitize instead of washing your hands with soap and water after caring for Jordan? Why or why not?

_____

_____

_____

_____

8. Should housekeeping be alerted to the fact that Jordan has C. Diff? Why or why not?

_____

_____

_____

_____

9. Jordan needs to have a chest X-ray this afternoon. They are on contact precautions. How should you get Jordan ready before they leave their room to go to the radiology department?

_____

_____

_____

_____

10. Is there anything else you need to do before transporting them? What might that be?

_____

_____

_____

_____

11. You have just finished helping Jordan in the restroom. Their condition has progressively gotten worse today. They are now incontinent of stool and bleeding rectally with each loose stool. Their incontinence product is soiled with feces and blood. How should you dispose of the product without contaminating yourself or others?

_____

_____

_____

_____

12. *Clostridium difficile* can lead to what complications?

_____

_____

_____

_____

6.C Fill in the blanks using terms found in the word bank.

barrier	1800s	antibody
lifestyle choices	staph	transmission
immunity	chain of infection	drug-resistant
primary prevention	susceptible host	infection control
healthcare workers	limiting	microorganisms
preventing	vaccine	enhanced barrier precautions

1. Infection control is _____ or _____ the spread of germs.

2. Personal protective equipment acts as a _____ between the healthcare worker and infectious agents.

3. _____ is preventing or limiting the spread of germs.

4. It is important for _____ to become vaccinated.

5. _____ is preventing the disease before it starts.

6. A(n) _____ is a body's defense against a specific invader.

7. If a resident has a diagnosis of an MDRO, an indwelling device, or a wound, _____ are used for all high contact activities.

8. A _____ is an individual who is at risk for infection.

9. Options for treating residents with _____ infections are very limited.

10. A bodily defense that prevents illness from occurring upon exposure to a specific germ is called _____.

11. Antibodies are produced by either a(n) _____ or exposure to the disease itself.

12. Mode of _____ is how germs move from one host to the next.

13. Germ theory is the idea that _____ are the cause of illness.

14. In the _____ people did not know about germs.

15. The _____ has six links.

16. Nonspecific defense mechanisms are helped or harmed by _____.

17. MRSA is a(n) _____ infection that has become resistant to many antibiotics.

6.D Multiple-Choice Exercises

1. Hand sanitizers must contain what percent alcohol to be effective?

   a) 5–15%
   b) 20–30%
   c) 40–65%
   d) 60–95%

2. One example of a fomite might be

   a) the healthcare worker's hands.
   b) bodily fluids.
   c) bedpans and urinals.
   d) an open area in the skin.

3. The medical community accepted the use of antiseptic solutions as a way to prevent the spread of disease after

   a) Semmelweis conducted experiments in the 1700s.
   b) Semmelweis made midwives wash their hands after delivery.
   c) Pasteur conducted experiments to prove germ theory.
   d) medical students were made to wash their hands before seeing residents.

4. Louis Pasteur was an inventor responsible for the pasteurization process and for developing a vaccine for

   a) rabies.
   b) measles.
   c) smallpox.
   d) tuberculosis.

5. You are assigned to care for Clarice, a resident with a respiratory infection. You must wear gloves when

   a) transporting Clarice to radiology.
   b) helping Clarice with their meal.
   c) helping Clarice into a clean gown.
   d) assisting Clarice with oral care.

6. The nursing assistant should remove their gloves

   a) when the gloves are visibly soiled.
   b) immediately after leaving a resident's room.
   c) when the resident requests them to do so.
   d) only when care for the resident is complete.

7. The MAIN reason a healthcare worker should be vaccinated against disease is that

   a) employers offer free vaccinations.
   b) the CDC requires all healthcare workers to be immunized.
   c) vaccines help protect the worker and their residents.
   d) vaccinations need to be complete to work as a nursing assistant.

8. One example of the body's nonspecific defense mechanisms would be

   a) immunizations.
   b) exposure to past illness.
   c) bacteria in the digestive tract.
   d) wearing the appropriate PPE.

9. Hand hygiene may be done using hand sanitizer in all of the following situations EXCEPT

   a) after using the restroom.
   b) after taking off gloves.
   c) before and after eating.
   d) when coming back from break.

10. Airborne precautions require the use of a(n)

    a) surgical mask if closer than 3 feet to the resident.
    b) particulate respirator (N95) mask.
    c) surgical mask and isolation gown.
    d) isolation gown and goggles.

11. The MOST important primary preventative measure against the spread of disease is to

    a) eat a healthy diet and exercise.
    b) get recommended vaccinations on schedule.
    c) see a healthcare provider as soon as you become ill.
    d) wash hands or use hand sanitizer consistently.

12. When caring for a resident who is on contact precautions for MRSA, you should use

    a) soap and water after resident contact.
    b) hand sanitizer before exiting the room.
    c) either soap and water OR hand sanitizer after providing care.
    d) soap and water only if the resident has a fever.

13. The benefits of performing hand hygiene include

    a) limiting the spread of illnesses from one resident to the next.
    b) reducing the risk of the healthcare worker becoming ill.
    c) controlling healthcare costs.
    d) all of the above.

14. The nursing assistant should wear gloves when

    a) feeding a resident in a common dining room.
    b) carrying linens from the linen closet to a resident's room.
    c) leaving a resident's room.
    d) washing a resident's face and hands.

15. Compared to washing with soap and water, using a hand sanitizer is

    a) more effective in killing germs.
    b) more time consuming.
    c) harder on the caregiver's skin.
    d) less effective against germs.

16. The PPE that a nursing assistant must wear when taking care of a resident is based upon the

    a) resident's abilities and needs.
    b) nursing assistant's risk of exposure.
    c) PPE available in the facility.
    d) resident's physical appearance.

17. An example of a staph infection that is resistant to a number of antibiotics is

    a) tuberculosis.
    b) MRSA.
    c) Clostridium difficile.
    d) VRE.

18. Thomas is taking care of a resident who has been placed on droplet precautions due to influenza. Before entering the resident's room, Thomas must put on a(n)

    a) N95 respirator.
    b) isolation gown, gloves, and goggles.
    c) surgical mask.
    d) gown and gloves.

19. VRE infections occur most often in

    a) hospitals.
    b) the community.
    c) long-term care facilities.
    d) the resident's home.

6.E   Choose the best response to the following scenarios.

1. Your resident has been admitted to the hospital a third time with an infection obtained during a previous hospital stay. The resident tells you it is the doctor's fault. What is the best response?

    a) Agree with the resident—you know the doctor has bad infection rates.
    b) Listen sympathetically and assure the resident you are there to help.
    c) Report the doctor to your direct supervisor.
    d) Say nothing—the resident does not understand how hospitals work.

2. Your employer offers you the flu vaccine, but you're unsure if you want the vaccination. What should you do?

    a) Try to avoid the situation as long as possible.
    b) Tell everyone how the employer is forcing you to become vaccinated.
    c) If indicated, receive the vaccination to help protect you and your residents from illness.
    d) Look for another job that doesn't require a flu shot.

3. You notice an older, more experienced nursing assistant not washing their hands after assisting their assigned residents with morning showers. What should you do?

    a) Ignore this, since they have more experience with providing care.
    b) Remind them of the importance of hand hygiene.
    c) Report them to your supervisor.
    d) Ask not to work with them.

4. You notice one of your coworkers exiting the bathroom without washing their hands. What is the best response?

    a) Politely remind them it is important that all healthcare workers wash hands after using the restroom.
    b) Tell your supervisor what you have witnessed.
    c) Refuse to work with them.
    d) Tell the coworker they must purchase hand sanitizer to use while working.

5. Your resident is upset and feels they are contaminated because everyone is wearing PPE when entering their room. What is your best response?

    a) Reassure them that the PPE is required to prevent the infection from spreading to others.
    b) Agree with them and take off your PPE once you are in the room.
    c) Tell the nurse to take them off of precautions—it is upsetting them.
    d) Ask to be reassigned because the resident is too emotionally exhausting.

6. You have just discovered that the resident you have been caring for all week is HIV-positive. What should you do?

    a) Ask the nurse to assign another nursing assistant to care for the resident.
    b) Talk with the resident and relay your feelings that you are upset with them for not reporting this to you.
    c) Carry out your duties as normal; you are safe because you use standard precautions when providing care.
    d) Request that the nurse supply you with isolation gowns, masks, gloves, and goggles in order to care for the resident safely.

7. You witness a coworker not wearing the proper PPE as indicated. When you remind them, they say, "I'm not worried about it. It takes too long to put on." What is the best response?

    a) Suggest they keep an isolation gown on during their entire shift and change gloves after leaving residents' rooms.

    b) Remind them that the extra time to put on the PPE is protecting themself and their resident.

    c) Tell them that the PPE is only required if they are bathing or toileting residents.

    d) Ask the director of nursing to have an in-service on proper PPE use.

8. You are in a hurry and forget to wash your hands after leaving a resident's room. What should you do?

    a) Only use hand sanitizer for the remainder of your shift.

    b) Do nothing and go to the next resident.

    c) Rub your hands on your uniform.

    d) Use your hand sanitizer before touching anything else.

This page intentionally left blank.

Module 7: Weights and Measures

7.A   Matching Definitions

No definitions listed in the module.

7.B   Reflective Short-Answer Exercises

Carlos is a 72-year-old resident with kidney failure. They were admitted to your facility this morning because they are no longer able to care for themself at home. Carlos is too weak to stand without assistance; they require a gait belt and an assist of one for transfers. The nurse asks you to obtain a full set of vital signs, weight, and height.

1.   Why would the nurse be requesting a height measurement?

_____

_____

_____

_____

2.   What method should you use to obtain Carlos's height?

_____

_____

_____

_____

3.   What could Carlos's weight indicate regarding their medical status?

_____

_____

_____

_____

4.   What is the best method to use when obtaining Carlos's weight?

_____

_____

_____

_____

7.C Fill in the blanks using terms found in the word bank.

metric   capacity   healthcare

milliliters   ambulatory   bath day

military time   Standard System   kilogram

illness

1. The Imperial System of measurement is sometimes referred to as the _____.

2. If a resident is not _____, you may need to measure their height in bed.

3. A resident's weight is measured on their scheduled _____ or during an illness as delegated by the nurse.

4. Volume measures _____.

5. Liquid volumes are typically documented in _____, but sometimes cubic centimeters are used.

6. _____ is based off a 24-hour cycle.

7. The metric system is used in _____ in the United States.

8. A change in weight can indicate _____, malnutrition, or overeating habits.

9. Measurements of smaller weight units in healthcare are most often noted in the _____ system.

10. One _____ equals 2.2 pounds.

7.D Multiple-Choice Exercises

1. The nurse must be updated with weights that show a gain or loss of how much from the resident's previous weight?

    a) 2 pounds or more
    b) 3 pounds or more
    c) 5 pounds or more
    d) greater than 10 pounds

2. A wall-mounted stadiometer is used to obtain a resident's

    a) weight if they can stand with assistance.
    b) height if they can stand independently.
    c) weight if they are wheelchair bound.
    d) height if they can stand with assistance.

3. One ounce of fluid equals

    a) 30 cc.
    b) 30 mL.
    c) 10 mL.
    d) both a and b.

4. Food items that must be calculated in a resident's total fluid intake include

    a) ice cream.
    b) sherbet.
    c) coffee.
    d) all of the above.

5. One of your residents has completed their meal, and you need to document their fluid intake. They drank 6 ounces of milk, 2 ounces of coffee, and 4 ounces of juice. The amount you should document is

    a) 12 ounces.
    b) 120 mL.
    c) 360 mL.
    d) 240 mL.

6. Urinary output is measured by using

   a) a graduate.
   b) a urinal.
   c) a bedpan.
   d) either a or b.

7. To obtain the weight of a resident who is unable to stand or sit up, you can use a(n)

   a) mechanical lift.
   b) wheelchair scale.
   c) upright scale.
   d) none of the above.

8. You are charting an incident that occurred at 6:30 that evening. When documenting, you should write that time as

   a) 6:30 PM.
   b) 06:30 PM.
   c) 1830.
   d) 18:30.

9. One of your residents is on a fluid restriction and needs all their fluid intake charted. You should document this information

   a) in the resident's chart after completion of meals and snacks, verifying the total at the end of the shift.
   b) on a paper flow sheet at the resident's bedside at the end of the shift.
   c) in the resident's chart only after each meal.
   d) only if they drink more than their fluid restriction allows.

10. When measuring urinary output, you should

   a) place the graduate on paper towels on the bathroom countertop.
   b) lift the graduate to eye level.
   c) read the measurement off the urinary drainage bag.
   d) place the graduate on paper towels on the overbed table.

7.E Choose the best response to the following scenarios.

1. Mrs. Lang is a resident with congestive heart failure. The doctor has ordered a new medication to help the body get rid of extra fluid. The nurse requested that Mrs. Lang's weight be obtained each morning to determine if the medication is effective. Mrs. Lang refuses to have their weight taken this morning. What is the best response?

   a) Instruct Mrs. Lang on the importance of daily weights.
   b) Ask Mrs. Lang why they don't want their weight taken and then update the nurse.
   c) Tell Mrs. Lang that they need to have their weight taken as directed.
   d) Reapproach Mrs. Lang later that night.

2. The nurse asks you to obtain the weight of a resident who was admitted to your facility that morning. The resident is non-weight bearing and has been bedridden for the past several months. Their last recorded weight was 412 pounds. What is the best option for obtaining the resident's weight?

   a) mechanical lift
   b) standing scale
   c) bariatric lift
   d) wheelchair scale

This page intentionally left blank.

Module 8: Patient Care Skill

8.A   Matching Definitions

_____ 1. Maceration

_____ 2. Prosthesis

_____ 3. Urostomy

_____ 4. Occult blood

_____ 5. Microclimate

_____ 6. Suppository

_____ 7. Friction/shearing prevention device

_____ 8. Urinary retention

_____ 9. Debridement

_____ 10. Ileostomy

_____ 11. Mastectomy

_____ 12. Orange stick

_____ 13. Colostomy

_____ 14. Frank blood

_____ 15. Stoma

_____ 16. Eschar

_____ 17. Shear

_____ 18. Oral swab

_____ 19. Bony prominence

_____ 20. Peri-care

_____ 21. Immobility

_____ 22. Friction

_____ 23. Alopecia

_____ 24. Orthosis

_____ 25. Paraphimosis

_____ 26. TED hose

A. A sponge attached to a small stick; used to clean the inside of the mouth

B. Washing the perineal area

C. The chemical or manual removal of eschar

D. A wax cone that is inserted into the rectum to aid in a bowel movement

E. The inability of the resident to move themselves purposefully

F. The movement of one layer of skin against another layer, or one layer of skin against a hard surface

G. The swelling that prevents the retraction of the foreskin back over the head of the penis

H. Hidden blood

I. The inability to partially or totally empty the bladder

J. A close environment in which heat and humidity are localized

K. Red, obvious blood

L. One end of the small intestine is drawn outside of the abdominal wall for the passage of stool

M. The ureters are detached from the bladder and then attached to a segment of bowel, one end of which extends outside the abdominal wall; allows urine to drain to the outside of the body

N. A loss of body hair, usually on the scalp

O. Skin that is softened from constant exposure to moisture

P. An artificial limb or body part; sometimes called a prosthetic

Q. A brace, splint, or orthopedic device

R. Tight, elastic stockings designed to prevent blood clots from forming in the legs

S. An opening that protrudes from the abdomen connecting an internal organ to the outside of the body

definitions continued on next page

T. A device used to move residents with the least amount of friction or shearing on the resident and the least amount of exertion for the nursing assistant

U. A small wooden stick with a pointed end and a wedged flat end; used during nail care

V. Any area of bone that sticks out or protrudes from the body

W. The complete or partial removal of the breast

X. A force on the skin; occurs when the body slides down in bed causing injury to the tissue

Y. One end of the large intestine is drawn outside of the abdominal wall for the passage of stool

Z. Necrotic tissue sometimes found in a pressure injury

8.B Reflective Short-Answer Exercises

Scenario 1:
Ida is a resident at the long-term care facility where you work. The last few days Ida has not been feeling well due to a urinary tract infection. Their symptoms of dementia are much more prominent. You are assigned to assist Ida with their tub bath this morning. Normally Ida enjoys their bath, but when you try to take them into the tub room, they start screaming and crying.

1. Why would Ida's bath be disturbing to them now when it has been a source of comfort in the past?

_____

_____

_____

_____

2. Should you continue with Ida's bath despite their behavior? Why or why not?

_____

_____

_____

_____

3. What alternatives could you use to limit Ida's distress during bathing?

_____

_____

_____

_____

4. How should you wash Ida's hair to minimize distress?

_____

_____

_____

_____

5. What other responsibilities might you have on a resident's bath day?

_____

_____

_____

_____

Scenario 2:

Carol is a 91-year-old resident with diabetes. They also have dementia, are unable to ambulate, and are incontinent of urine and feces. When you are bathing them today, you notice a red area on their bottom. The area is not open, but the redness doesn't go away after you bathe and reposition Carol. You ask them if the area hurts, and they say no. After their bath, you dress them and help them into their wheelchair using a gait belt and assist of another nurse aide. When you are assisting them with their breakfast, they state they only want to eat desserts.

1. Why do you think Carol might not feel any pain on the reddened area on their bottom?

_____

_____

_____

_____

2. Does Carol have a pressure injury on their bottom? If so, what stage would it be?

_____

_____

_____

_____

3. Should you report the reddened area to the nurse? When should you do this?

_____

_____

_____

_____

4. What would put Carol at risk for skin breakdown?

_____

_____

_____

_____

5. How could Carol's incontinence be affecting the skin on their bottom?

_____

_____

_____

6. How often should you be repositioning Carol?

_____

_____

_____

7. How often should you be changing Carol's incontinence product and performing peri-care?

_____

_____

_____

8. What product should be used for cleaning the peri-area?

_____

_____

_____

9. What other interventions can you do to help heal the pressure injury on Carol's bottom?

_____

_____

_____

10. Would you get Carol extra desserts today and only feed them those? Why or why not?

_____

_____

_____

_____

8.C   Fill in the blanks using terms found in the word bank.

rashes	partially bathed	challenge
privacy	urethra	every night
affected	direction	skin
anti-embolism	independent	two
rinseless	humidity	shearing
hydration	prevention	abdomen
empathetic	nails	sock
elimination	hemorrhoids	incontinence garment
alternatives	supplies	soft cloth
constipation		

1. _____ soap is an effective, efficient, and gentle way to cleanse residents.

2. The _____ is the cleanest part of the perineum.

3. Before beginning the bath, prepare a clean and easily accessible space on which to place your _____.

4. Assisting residents with _____ needs, such as toileting and changing incontinence products, is a large part of the nursing assistant role.

5. Each resident should be _____ twice each day, with the exception of their shower or tub bath day.

6. Resident bathing can be a _____ for those who have dementia.

7. A resident who slides down in bed is at risk of _____, which causes injury to the skin.

8. TED hose are also called _____ stockings.

9. An orange stick is a small wooden stick with a sharp pointed end and a wedged flat end used for cleaning beneath the resident's _____.

10. We should encourage residents to be as _____ as possible to maintain strength and mobility.

11. A stoma is an opening that protrudes from the _____ and connects an internal organ to the outside of the body.

12. It is important to always check the resident's _____ while you bathe them.

13. If a resident is totally dependent on you for elimination needs, you will have to change their _____ every 2 hours.

14. When assisting a resident with dressing, you should offer at least _____ outfits for the resident to choose between.

15. _____ are large distended veins found in and around the anus.

16. When dressing a resident who suffers from one-sided paralysis, you should always begin by inserting the resident's _____ side into the shirtsleeve first.

17. To prevent scratching the lenses, clean glasses with a _____.

18. Shave a man's face in the _____ of hair growth when using a disposable razor.

19. During bathing, be _____ and sincere in your caring so that the resident is more comfortable.

20. There are _____ to traditional tub bathing or showering that can make bathing more comfortable for residents with dementia.

21. Oral care should be performed every morning and _____.

22. Microclimate is related to the heat and _____ between a resident's skin and the bed or wheelchair.

23. As a nursing assistant, _____ of skin breakdown is your responsibility.

24. A resident with an artificial limb has either a _____ or a gel insert to help protect the skin beneath the prosthesis.

25. Having to strain to have a bowel movement and having infrequent bowel movements is defined as _____.

26. Sometimes skin _____ are an overgrowth of yeast, causing a yeast infection.

27. _____ and proper protein intake is very important to maintaining healthy skin.

28. Always provide _____ when bathing a resident.

8.D   Multiple-Choice Exercises

1. Peri-care should be completed

    a) each morning when the resident wakes.
    b) every evening before going to bed.
    c) after changing a soiled incontinence garment.
    d) all of the above.

2. When using an electric razor with three rotating heads, you should shave the resident's face

    a) in the direction of hair growth.
    b) against the direction of hair growth.
    c) in small, rotating circles.
    d) in large circles until smooth.

3. Healthy, intact skin helps to

    a) regulate body temperature.
    b) protect the body from germs.
    c) maintain moisture levels in the body.
    d) do all of the above.

4. You should clean a resident's eyeglasses by using

    a) dry paper towels.
    b) a soft cloth.
    c) glass cleaner and paper towels.
    d) warm water and facial tissues.

5. A partial bed bath includes all the following areas of the body EXCEPT

    a) under breasts.
    b) the peri-area.
    c) under abdominal folds.
    d) arms.

6. A complete bed bath typically begins with the resident's

    a) hands.
    b) face.
    c) chest.
    d) peri-area.

7. Female peri-care should be completed by cleansing the area from

    a) front to back, starting at the urethra.
    b) front to back, starting with the groin and upper thigh.
    c) back to front, starting at the urethra.
    d) back to front, starting with the anus.

8. Your resident's care plan states they should be repositioned every 2 hours. They refuse to allow you to reposition them, even after many attempts. What should you do?

a) Respect their wishes.
b) Reposition them as stated in their care plan.
c) Report their refusal to the nurse.
d) Ask their family to explain the need for repositioning.

9. After a resident wakes, the FIRST thing you typically assist them with is

a) getting dressed.
b) a partial bed bath or shower.
c) oral care.
d) range-of-motion exercises.

10. Agnes is a resident who has left-sided weakness due to a stroke. When getting Agnes dressed, you should

a) put their left arm into the sleeve first, while supporting the arm.
b) put their right arm into the sleeve first.
c) put their shirt over their head first, followed by their right arm.
d) put both arms into the sleeves, and then pull the shirt over their head.

11. When assisting with a resident's shower, you should wash the hair

a) first, and then proceed to the face and body.
b) last, so the resident does not get cold.
c) either first or last, whichever the resident prefers.
d) none of the above; all residents have their hair done in the beauty shop.

12. For a resident who takes a whirlpool tub bath, peri-care is completed

a) by the action of the whirlpool tub.
b) while they are in the tub by stooping next to them.
c) in their room before the tub bath.
d) none of the above; peri-care is not done.

13. Lotion should NOT be applied to a resident's

a) feet.
b) back.
c) abdominal folds.
d) chest.

14. Coral is scheduled to have their shower this morning. They often get cold during their shower, but there are no clean bath blankets available. You should

a) use a bed blanket to cover them during the shower.
b) wait for the laundry service to bring clean bath blankets.
c) ask the next shift to give Coral their shower.
d) explain to Coral that you will finish the shower as quickly as possible.

15. Clara is a resident who is incontinent. While bathing them this morning, you notice a dime-sized open area on one of their buttocks. Your FIRST step should be to

a) clean the area with adult wipes and apply barrier cream.
b) make sure that Clara is covered and safe, and then ask the nurse to look at the area.
c) get Clara dressed and then tell the nurse about the open area.
d) sprinkle powder in the clean brief to absorb moisture.

16. For a resident who is unconscious, you should provide oral care by using a(n)

a) soft-bristled toothbrush.
b) oral swab.
c) gauze-covered tongue depressor.
d) moistened piece of gauze.

17. When using a disposable razor to shave a resident's face, you should shave

a) in the direction of hair growth.
b) in a circular pattern.
c) in the opposite direction of hair growth.
d) either in the direction of hair growth or in a circular pattern.

18. You have put your resident's hearing aids in for them, but they are still unable to hear. The FIRST thing you should do is

    a) ensure the battery compartment is closed.
    b) ask the nurse for new batteries.
    c) inform the nurse that the resident's hearing aids do not work.
    d) check to ensure that the volume is turned up.

19. The nursing assistant should line the sink with a barrier during denture care in order to

    a) prevent germs from getting on the dentures.
    b) prevent damage to the dentures if they are dropped.
    c) keep the surfaces of the sink clean.
    d) have a clean area to set the dentures down.

20. Otto is a resident who has diabetes. Today is their bath day, and they need to have their nail care done. You should

    a) ask an experienced nursing assistant to trim their nails.
    b) clean, trim, and file their fingernails.
    c) ask the nurse to trim their fingernails.
    d) have the occupational therapist provide nail care.

21. The water temperature of a whirlpool tub bath should be between

    a) 100°F and 104°F.
    b) 90°F and 100°F.
    c) 75°F and 85°F.
    d) 105°F and 110°F.

22. Pine or tar products are added to a medicinal bath for a resident with

    a) psoriasis.
    b) inflammation in the peri-area.
    c) arthritis.
    d) a skin infection.

23. A rash found under a resident's arms may be the result of

    a) shearing.
    b) pressure.
    c) infection.
    d) debridement.

24. You are assisting a resident to the toilet and notice that they have an open area on their coccyx. You should

    a) clean the area and apply barrier cream.
    b) immediately report your findings to the nurse.
    c) place a cushion in the resident's wheelchair.
    d) apply a small amount of powder or cornstarch.

25. You need to provide oral care for an unconscious resident. You can open their mouth by using

    a) your gloved hand.
    b) a dry oral swab.
    c) the resident's toothbrush.
    d) a gauze-wrapped wooden tongue depressor.

26. A prosthesis may be used to replace a body part that is lost or removed due to

    a) vascular disease.
    b) frostbite.
    c) a birth defect.
    d) all of the above.

27. Preventable skin rashes most often appear

    a) across the chest and abdomen.
    b) beneath breasts, under arms, and between skin folds.
    c) on the legs and feet.
    d) on the face, neck, and ears.

28. The factor that places the resident MOST at risk of developing a pressure injury is

    a) dementia.
    b) inability to sense pain.
    c) incontinence.
    d) immobility.

29. An intact area on the coccyx that is red, painful, and has edema would be a

    a) stage-one pressure injury.
    b) stage-two pressure injury.
    c) stage-three pressure injury.
    d) stage-four pressure injury.

30. Bathing with a rinseless system instead of soap and water

    a) is more time consuming.
    b) is gentler on the resident's skin.
    c) means the skin is not as clean.
    d) is not appropriate for older residents.

31. Ellen is an older resident who is immobile and does not have much of an appetite. Because they are at risk of developing pressure injuries, it is MOST important for them to eat

    a) fruits.
    b) grains.
    c) proteins.
    d) vegetables.

32. A resident who is incontinent should be assisted to the toilet

    a) twice in an 8-hour shift.
    b) once in the morning and once in the evening.
    c) every 2 hours.
    d) every hour while awake.

33. Immobile residents must be repositioned

    a) every 2 hours while in bed.
    b) every hour when in a wheelchair.
    c) every 2 hours while the resident is awake.
    d) both a and b.

34. Maceration of a resident's skin is likely to result from

    a) repositioning without using a lift sheet.
    b) not changing an incontinence garment when soiled.
    c) not offering snacks and fluids between meals.
    d) placing an alternating-pressure mattress on the bed.

35. Elmer is a resident recovering from a hip replacement. They tell you that they need to use the bathroom to have a bowel movement. Their care plan states that they are an assist of two for transfers, but you are unable to find a coworker to help you. You should

    a) offer them a fracture pan.
    b) offer them a traditional bedpan.
    c) ask if they can wait until you find help.
    d) offer to help them use a bedside commode.

36. You are caring for a resident who needs to be repositioned, but there are no lift sheets available. You should

    a) use a folded top sheet as a lift sheet.
    b) ask them to pull themself up in bed using the side rails.
    c) reposition them by lifting underneath their arms.
    d) tell the nurse that you are unable to reposition the resident.

37. When emptying a colostomy bag, the nursing assistant should clean the skin around the stoma with

    a) damp paper towels.
    b) alcohol wipes.
    c) adult wipes.
    d) ostomy powder.

38. The nursing assistant must check the skin beneath a resident's prosthesis

    a) once a week on bath day.
    b) at least once every three days.
    c) before placing and after removal of the prosthesis.
    d) once per day in the morning.

39. Caring for the skin beneath a prosthesis includes

    a) cleaning with mild soap and water daily.
    b) shaving the area every day.
    c) applying lotion to keep the skin moist.
    d) soaking the residual limb in warm water for comfort.

40. Javier often becomes upset and agitated when given their weekly shower. They find it cold and painful. You should

    a) offer a complete bed bath in place of the shower.
    b) keep them covered with a bath blanket or towels.
    c) provide a partial bed bath instead of a shower.
    d) both a and b.

8.E Choose the best response to the following scenarios.

1. A resident has had a large loose bowel movement in their incontinence garment while sitting in the common dining room with other residents. What should you do?

    a) Allow them to finish eating in the dining room and then take them to their room to provide peri-care.
    b) Take them and their meal to their room and perform peri-care when they are done eating breakfast.
    c) Discreetly take them to their room, provide peri-care, and then assist them back to the dining room.
    d) Allow them to finish breakfast and then provide peri-care in the closest bathroom.

2. Thomas is a resident you are caring for this morning. It is their scheduled shower day, but they have refused. They state that they don't like to take showers. What should you do?

    a) Offer an alternative such as a bed bath.
    b) Do nothing; they have the right to refuse.
    c) Explain to Thomas that they need to shower to keep their skin healthy.
    d) Ask the nurse to schedule their showers for a different day.

3. You need to complete a resident's partial bed bath but only have two washcloths available. What should you do?

    a) Bathe the resident using the two washcloths, making sure to wash from cleanest areas first, and providing peri-care last.
    b) Provide peri-care only.
    c) Use another resident's clean washcloths.
    d) Use paper towels from the dispenser to dry the skin.

4. Your male resident has asked you to help them apply their makeup. What should you do?

    a) Tell them that it is not appropriate.
    b) Help them apply the makeup.
    c) Update their family regarding the request.
    d) Suggest that they not put makeup on today.

5. You are assigned to care for two residents who reside in the same room. Both residents are named Mary, wear glasses, and suffer from dementia. You are unsure whose glasses belong to whom. What should you do?

    a) See which pair of glasses fits each resident.
    b) Ask the residents to identify their glasses.
    c) Ask the nurse to identify the glasses.
    d) Call each resident's family to describe the glasses.

6. A resident that you have cared for has a pressure injury. The nurse begins an investigation to determine how and when the pressure injury developed. You have provided skin care as directed in the resident's care plan. When the nurse questions you, what is the best response?

    a) Explain that it was not your fault; other nursing assistants had cared for the resident too.
    b) Tell the nurse that you have followed the care plan and that your charting reflects this.
    c) Update the nurse that the resident has been eating poorly lately and that this may be the reason for the injury.
    d) Tell the nurse you think the nursing assistants on the night shift are not providing appropriate skin care.

7. Your resident asks you to apply lotion between their toes after foot care. What should you do?

   a) Apply lotion between their toes as requested.
   b) Explain that it is not within your scope of practice.
   c) Ask the nurse for baby powder to use instead of lotion.
   d) Report the resident's request to the nurse and ask for directives.

8. You notice a reddened area on your resident's right heel that was not there yesterday. What should you do FIRST?

   a) Report the pressure injury to the nurse.
   b) Ask your coworkers if they noticed the reddened area.
   c) Place the heel on two pillows.
   d) Watch the area to make sure it does not get worse.

9. A resident has requested their colostomy bag be changed before they leave their room for the day. Their roommate is having breakfast on the other side of the room. What would you do?

   a) Change the bag in the room as the resident requests.
   b) Ask the resident to wait until their roommate is finished with breakfast.
   c) Assist the resident to a bathroom and then change the bag.
   d) Take the breakfast away from the roommate while you change the bag.

10. Your resident has been up in their wheelchair for 2 hours and does not want to lie in bed or sit in their recliner. Their care plan says to reposition them every 2 hours. What should you do?

    a) Help them to stand or ambulate.
    b) Put them in the recliner near the nurses' desk.
    c) Assist them back into bed.
    d) Place them in front of the television.

11. You notice that your coworker is not offering fluids to the residents, and you're concerned that they may become dehydrated. What should you do?

    a) Make sure you offer extra fluids to make up for it.
    b) Report your coworker to the supervisor immediately.
    c) Understand that this may take extra time that your coworker doesn't have.
    d) Remind your coworker of the importance of hydration.

12. You enter a resident's room to find them crying. They tell you they are upset because of hair loss caused by their cancer treatments. What should you do?

    a) Tell them that you understand and then leave the room to provide privacy.
    b) Suggest that they purchase a wig or scarf to cover their head.
    c) Allow the resident to express their feelings and then report this to the nurse.
    d) Tell them that it is only a temporary hair loss; it will grow back soon.

13. Your resident who is normally continent has had a loose, incontinent bowel movement while in bed. They are very embarrassed and upset. What should you do?

    a) Place an incontinent garment on them to prevent more accidents.
    b) Remind them that they should call for assistance quicker next time they need to use the bathroom.
    c) Clean them up in a caring and professional manner and place clean linens on their bed.
    d) Put them on the commode every 2 hours for the rest of your shift.

14. A male resident's family has brought a package of disposable razors to the facility for them to use. The resident has asked you to help them with shaving this morning. What should you do?

    a) Help them shave and keep the package of razors in their room for the next time.
    b) Explain to the resident that disposable razors are not allowed in long-term care facilities.
    c) Suggest the resident call their family for an electric razor instead.
    d) Verify with the care plan that they may use disposable razors.

15. While changing your resident's colostomy bag, you become nauseated from the smell. What should you do?

    a) Tell the resident you are becoming ill.
    b) Refuse to change the ostomy bag next time.
    c) Do your best to finish the task in a professional manner.
    d) Ask another nursing assistant to complete the task.

16. You are assisting a resident with toileting and need to change their incontinence garment. They normally wear a small size, but you are only able to find garments labeled as large. What should you do?

    a) Change the resident into the large incontinence garment, ensure comfort and adequate fit, and then update the nurse.
    b) Borrow from another resident who uses similar incontinence products and then update the nurse.
    c) Have the resident remain in bed until small-sized incontinence garments can be purchased.
    d) Ask the nurse to insert a catheter until the facility can purchase more supplies.

17. You are instructed to reposition your resident with three pillows. You only have two. What should you do?

    a) Use only the two that you have.
    b) Borrow one of the roommate's pillows.
    c) Call the family to purchase more pillows.
    d) Roll a bath blanket to use as a positioning device.

Module 9: Patient Care Procedures

9.A   Matching Definitions

_____ 1. Urinary analysis

_____ 2. Occupied bed change

_____ 3. Reusable incontinence pad

_____ 4. Suprapubic catheter

_____ 5. Closed bed

_____ 6. Bath blanket

_____ 7. Acute condition

_____ 8. Chronic condition

_____ 9. Linens

_____ 10. Open bed

_____ 11. Ambulatory surgery

_____ 12. Atelectasis

_____ 13. Splinting

_____ 14. Incentive spirometer

A. A bed made with the top sheet, blanket, and bedspread fanfolded down to the foot or side of the bed

B. A process that decreases pain by supporting the chest and abdomen during coughing and deep breathing

C. The bedding that covers the mattress

D. A surgical procedure that does not require an overnight stay

E. A short-lived new injury or illness, which may or may not be resolved

F. A test that looks for bacteria in the urine

G. A bed made with all the linens in place over the mattress and drawn up to the head of the bed

H. A respiratory disorder in which gas exchange is limited due to either alveoli collapse or fluid buildup, causing chest pain, coughing, and sometimes respiratory distress

I. A medical device used to maintain lung function, or as an aid during respiratory illness

J. A disease, illness, or injury that lasts for a long period of time

K. A lightweight blanket used to cover residents for warmth and privacy while providing care

L. A pad that is placed under the resident to protect bed linens

M. A catheter that is inserted into the bladder through an opening in the abdomen

N. A change of bed linens when the resident is not able to get out of bed, or when it is uncomfortable for the resident to get out of bed

9.B Reflective Short-Answer Exercises

Scenario 1:

Roland is having problems urinating today, is weak, and needs more assistance during transfers than usual. They have also been telling stories of seeing people in their room at night. The nurse asks you to obtain a urine specimen from Roland.

1. What specific directives would you need to get from the nurse before obtaining a sample from Roland?

_____

_____

_____

_____

2. What type of specimen do you think you may have to obtain from Roland and why?

_____

_____

_____

_____

3. How would you obtain a urine specimen from Roland?

_____

_____

_____

_____

4. How would you ensure that the urine specimen wasn't contaminated?

_____

_____

_____

_____

Scenario 2:

Mario is a 29-year-old quadriplegic. They require assistance with bathing, eating, and mobility. They are incontinent of bowel and have an indwelling catheter, which they find embarrassing. Today you find that the area around the catheter is bleeding.

1. Is Mario at high risk for skin breakdown? Why or why not?

_____

_____

_____

_____

2. Where would you attach Mario's catheter holder?

_____

_____

_____

3. If a catheter holder were not available, what would you do?

_____

_____

_____

_____

4. How often would the catheter need to be cleaned? What steps do you take in providing this care?

_____

_____

_____

_____

5. What supplies would you need to empty the urinary collection bag and measure their urine output appropriately?

_____

_____

_____

_____

Scenario 3:
AJ is a resident who had a fall and is now staying in bed more and refusing to participate in activities. Today they are coughing, have a fever, and are found to have pneumonia.

1. Does AJ have an acute or chronic respiratory illness?

_____

_____

_____

_____

2. Why do you think they developed pneumonia?

_____

_____

_____

3. AJ now has an order for oxygen via nasal cannula at 2 liters per minute. The nurse brings an oxygen concentrator to AJ's room and turns it on to 2 liters per minute. What additional nursing assistant responsibilities do you have now that AJ has oxygen?

_____

_____

_____

_____

4. How would you maintain the oxygen concentrator in AJ's room to ensure that it is working properly?

    _____

    _____

    _____

    _____

5. What can you do to help ease any anxiety AJ may experience due to shortness of breath from the pneumonia?

    _____

    _____

    _____

    _____

6. What two exercises may be ordered to help resolve AJ's pneumonia?

    _____

    _____

    _____

    _____

7. What are the nursing assistant's responsibilities regarding these exercises?

    _____

    _____

    _____

    _____

Scenario 4:

Loretta is recovering from a car accident and has had multiple surgeries to their chest and abdomen. They have an IV running continuously and are NPO. You are responsible for applying sequential stockings and repositioning them every 2 hours.

1. Would Loretta be a medical or a surgical resident?

    _____

    _____

    _____

2. Why would Loretta be NPO?

    _____

    _____

    _____

3. When could they advance past NPO status?

    _____

    _____

    _____

4. What is Loretta's activity level at this point?

_____

_____

_____

_____

5. What respiratory complications is Loretta at risk for, and why?

_____

_____

_____

_____

6. What cardiac complications is Loretta at risk for, and why?

_____

_____

_____

_____

7. What will the sequential stockings do for them?

_____

_____

_____

_____

8. What would you have to be aware of when repositioning Loretta?

_____

_____

_____

_____

9.C Fill in the blanks using terms found in the word bank.

blood clots	contamination	cylinders
lift sheet	bath	clean
deep breathing	biohazard	bedpan
resist	nasal cannula	personal protective equipment
strain	indwelling catheter	catheter holder
face mask	nosebleeds	anxious
fecal samples	physician	drug

1. To avoid _____ while collecting the urine for a UA, first clean the resident's peri-area.

2. You may be required to _____ all urine for residents suffering from kidney stones.

3. _____ are sometimes necessary when the resident suffers from digestive problems or a diarrheal illness.

4. Your resident may become _____ or irritable when they are having difficulty breathing.

5. Remember to always wear appropriate _____ when collecting urine or fecal specimens.

6. Some residents may require a(n) _____, which stays in the bladder for a long period of time.

7. Never obtain a clean catch urine sample from a _____, urinal, or commode because it will alter the results of the urinalysis.

8. A(n) _____ can be used to deliver higher amounts of concentrated oxygen.

9. Postsurgical residents may _____ activity because of the pain.

10. After a sample is collected, it must be placed in a _____ bag.

11. Coughing and _____ exercises can help maintain the resident's lung function by expanding the lung tissue and clearing the lungs of mucus.

12. Oxygen is a _____ and therefore cannot be legally administered by the nursing assistant.

13. A(n) _____ is a long plastic tube with nasal prongs at the end of it, which delivers low doses of oxygen to the resident.

14. One side effect of continuous oxygen usage is _____.

15. TED hose are tight elastic stockings designed to help prevent _____ from forming in the legs.

16. It is the nursing assistant's responsibility to keep the resident's skin healthy by ensuring the bed linens are _____ and dry.

17. Oxygen can be stored in small and large metal _____.

18. Activity level for the resident is determined by the _____, nurse, and therapy team.

19. In long-term care facilities, bed linens are typically changed once or twice each week, on the same day as the resident's _____.

20. A(n) _____ is used when moving the resident up in the bed or over to the side of the bed during positioning.

21. A(n) _____ is a device used to decrease the amount of pulling on the catheter and thus trauma to the urethra and bladder.

9.D Multiple-Choice Exercises

1. When changing bed linens, the nursing assistant must wear gloves

   a) only when removing linens that are wet.
   b) when putting new linens on the bed.
   c) when removing any linens from the bed.
   d) during none of the above.

2. Calcium alginate dressings are used for

   a) skin tears.
   b) blisters.
   c) wounds with limited drainage.
   d) wounds with moderate drainage.

3. Good body mechanics include all of the following EXCEPT

    a) raising the bed to a good working height.
    b) keeping items close to your body.
    c) lowering side rails while you work.
    d) bending at the waist.

4. When a resident is ready to go to bed, the linens should be

    a) fanfolded to one side of the bed.
    b) fanfolded to the bottom of the bed.
    c) rolled down to the bottom of the bed.
    d) drawn up to the head of the bed.

5. Mattress pads are never used in

    a) hospitals.
    b) home healthcare.
    c) assisted-living facilities.
    d) residential care apartment complexes.

6. Kidney stones are collected by

    a) placing a commode hat in the front half of the toilet.
    b) straining the urine from the toilet.
    c) placing a specimen cup under the resident.
    d) placing a commode hat in the back half of the toilet.

7. The FIRST step in collecting a urine sample is to

    a) assemble your supplies.
    b) label the specimen container.
    c) put on your gown and gloves.
    d) verify the amount of urine needed.

8. You need to make an occupied bed for one of your residents. The bed does not have side rails. What should you do?

    a) Make the bed while it is in the low position.
    b) Roll the resident toward you while making the bed.
    c) Tell the resident that they must get out of bed.
    d) Move the bed against the wall and reach over the resident.

9. Before receiving an enema, a resident should be

    a) lying on their right side in bed.
    b) sitting on a toilet or commode.
    c) lying on their left side in bed.
    d) lying on their back with the head of the bed up.

10. Urine specimens may be collected to

    a) check for sugar levels.
    b) determine kidney function.
    c) measure potassium levels.
    d) do all of the above.

11. You are changing the linens on an alternating-pressure bed for a resident who is incontinent. The best option to place on the bed to prevent the linens from becoming soiled is a

    a) reusable incontinence pad.
    b) mattress pad.
    c) disposable incontinence pad.
    d) draw sheet.

12. The nursing assistant should make a closed bed when a resident is

    a) admitted to the hospital.
    b) ready to get into bed.
    c) up for the day.
    d) transferred from a stretcher.

13. While making an occupied bed, the side rails should be raised

    a) on the side the resident is rolling toward.
    b) on the side where you are working.
    c) never; side rails are a restraint.
    d) on both sides until you are finished.

14. An appropriate dressing to use for a resident with a skin tear is a

    a) transparent dressing.
    b) foam dressing.
    c) wet to dry dressing.
    d) gauze sponge.

15. When making an occupied bed, the nursing assistant should have the bed

    a) at about waist height.
    b) in the lowest position.
    c) against the wall.
    d) unlocked when rolling the resident.

16. Dory is a resident with COPD who requires supplementary oxygen. Today they have been using their call light every 15 minutes for small tasks. You try to tend to their needs, but they just become more anxious. You should

    a) have another nursing assistant take over Dory's care.
    b) take more breaks to reduce stress.
    c) inform the nurse of Dory's anxiety right away.
    d) tell the nurse about Dory's behavior at the end of your shift.

17. When collecting a stool sample, the nursing assistant should make sure that the sample is

    a) taken from a new commode or bedpan.
    b) not contaminated with toilet paper.
    c) not contaminated with urine.
    d) all of the above.

18. The MOST important reason for collection of kidney stones is to

    a) verify that stones are present.
    b) determine what the stones are made of.
    c) decrease the resident's discomfort.
    d) see what the stones look like.

19. The nursing assistant's scope of practice includes

    a) changing sterile bandages.
    b) applying barrier creams to intact skin.
    c) applying prescription ointments to intact skin.
    d) determining the appropriate dressing type for a wound.

20. You have obtained a stool specimen to check for occult blood. The FIRST step in using the fecal occult blood test kit is to

    a) close window A and B; open the back flap of the slide.
    b) apply two drops of developer solution to window A and B.
    c) apply a drop of developer solution to the control window.
    d) apply a thin smear of stool to windows A and B on the slide.

21. Doreen is a resident who is given an oral laxative for constipation. If they are unable to have a bowel movement after taking the laxative, the nurse is likely to administer a(n)

    a) soap suds enema.
    b) over-the-counter enema.
    c) suppository.
    d) liquid stool softener.

22. An indwelling catheter should be cleaned by

    a) moving the washcloth up and down the catheter until clean.
    b) starting closest to the body and moving downward about 4 inches.
    c) starting farthest from the body and moving upward about 4 inches.
    d) starting closest to the body and moving downward about 8 inches.

23. One of your residents is on oxygen at 2 liters per minute via a nasal cannula. Their oxygen tubing is connected to the concentrator in their room. This afternoon they are asking to go for a walk. You should

    a) ask the nurse to change the resident over to a portable tank and check the flow rate.
    b) push the concentrator down the hallway with them.
    c) remove their oxygen while you ambulate them.
    d) ask the nurse to ambulate them.

24. For chronic conditions, the flow rate of supplementary oxygen is typically

    a) 8–10 liters per minute.
    b) 6–8 liters per minute.
    c) 10–12 liters per minute.
    d) 1–6 liters per minute.

25. You have been assigned to obtain a stool specimen from one of your residents. After they have a bowel movement, you should take a sample from

    a) both ends and the middle of the stool.
    b) the middle of the stool only.
    c) both ends of the stool only.
    d) one end of the stool only.

26. You gather linens to change Sarah's bed. After you are in Sarah's room, you notice that you brought an extra fitted sheet. What should you do with the extra sheet?

    a) Return it to the linen closet.
    b) Place it in the soiled linen bag.
    c) Take it to the next resident's room to use.
    d) Set it on the floor while you make the bed.

27. One of your residents requires oxygen at night while they sleep. When you are placing the nasal cannula on them, the FIRST step should be

    a) inserting the cannula with the prongs facing the resident.
    b) placing the tubing loop over the resident's ears.
    c) verifying that the oxygen supply is on.
    d) bringing the sliding connector toward the resident's chin.

28. Mateo is a resident who is on oxygen via a nasal cannula. Today they tell you that their nose is stuffy and dry. You should update the nurse and

    a) place petroleum jelly in their nostrils.
    b) place distilled water in their concentrator.
    c) watch for nosebleeds.
    d) both b and c.

29. You can assist a resident with maintaining lung function by

    a) reinforcing coughing and deep breathing exercises.
    b) teaching the resident how to use an incentive spirometer.
    c) starting the resident on oxygen if they become short of breath.
    d) turning up the oxygen flow rate if the resident is anxious.

30. Typical nursing assistant responsibilities when caring for medical residents include

    a) drawing a resident's blood for lab tests.
    b) taking vital signs every 4 hours.
    c) administering a resident's insulin.
    d) inserting a urinary catheter.

31. You are walking past one of your resident's rooms when you hear their oxygen concentrator alarm beeping. You should

    a) ensure that the concentrator's filter is clean.
    b) refill the concentrator with oxygen.
    c) check how much oxygen is in the concentrator.
    d) call the resident's oxygen supplier.

32. A resident who is scheduled for ambulatory surgery can expect to

    a) be discharged to their home the same day as the surgery.
    b) remain in the hospital overnight.
    c) be discharged to a nursing home for rehabilitation.
    d) check in to the hospital the night before the surgery.

33. Elsa is a resident who had surgery on their left shoulder this morning. They tell you that they are thirsty and would like something to drink. You should

    a) offer them apple juice.
    b) offer them a glass of water.
    c) check their care plan for their current dietary status.
    d) tell them that they are unable to drink anything.

34. Jonathan is a postsurgical resident who is on a full-liquid diet. When you enter their room, they are drinking some orange juice. They tell you that they "feel like throwing up." You should

    a) inform the nurse that Jonathan drank orange juice and is now feeling nauseous.
    b) offer them something else to drink like white soda or apple juice.
    c) explain that nausea is common after surgery and that it will pass.
    d) offer them soda crackers to decrease the nausea.

35. The nurse has asked you to obtain a stool guaiac specimen. This test is used to check for

    a) bacteria.
    b) frank blood.
    c) occult blood.
    d) parasites.

36. Urinary output should be documented in a resident's chart

    a) at the end of the shift.
    b) only if there is a difference between intake and output.
    c) only if the resident has a urinary catheter.
    d) each time the resident uses the bathroom.

37. The weight-bearing status of a surgical resident is determined by the resident's

    a) nurse.
    b) surgeon.
    c) physical therapist.
    d) occupational therapist.

38. You are assigned to care for Leo, a 65-year-old resident with pneumonia. The nurse has directed you to assist Leo with their incentive spirometer. You will need to read Leo's care plan to

    a) check if they will be using the spirometer when they go home.
    b) verify how often they should use the spirometer.
    c) check that they have a doctor's order for the spirometer.
    d) get directions on how to use their spirometer.

39. Coughing and deep breathing exercises help the resident by

    a) eliminating germs in the lungs.
    b) expanding the lung tissue.
    c) clearing the lungs of mucus.
    d) doing both b and c.

40. One of your residents is recovering from right knee replacement surgery. The care plan states that their status is 25% weight bearing. This means that they can

    a) put 75% of their weight on their right leg.
    b) put 25% of their weight on their right leg.
    c) only toe touch on the right side.
    d) put weight on their right leg as tolerated.

41. Edna is a resident who had heart surgery 2 days ago. The nurse taught them how to do cough and deep breathing exercises, but they tell you they don't want to do the exercises because they are afraid that it will hurt. You should

    a) tell them that they can use an incentive spirometer instead.
    b) suggest that they wait a few more days before starting the exercises.
    c) encourage them to splint while performing the exercises.
    d) report their refusal to the respiratory therapist.

42. You are assigned to care for a surgical resident who has an IV in their left hand. They have asked to wear their own gown. You should

    a) bring the IV bag through the left sleeve first, followed by the left arm.
    b) bring their right arm through the right sleeve first, followed by the left.
    c) bring their left arm through the left sleeve first, followed by the IV bag.
    d) suggest they wear a hospital gown with snaps instead.

43. When placing sequential stockings under a resident's leg, you should make sure that

    a) the vinyl side of the stocking is against the resident's skin.
    b) you can slide four fingers between the stocking and leg.
    c) the flow rate is adjusted as indicated on the resident's care plan.
    d) you fasten the Velcro® of the stocking starting at the thigh.

44. The BEST time to put on a resident's TED hose is

    a) before they get out of bed.
    b) when they are sitting in their chair.
    c) right after their shower.
    d) when they go to bed at night.

45. A resident's notice of discharge from a facility must include

    a) date of discharge.
    b) the ombudsman's contact information.
    c) information on bed-hold policies.
    d) all of the above.

46. Joseph is a surgical resident who is on strict bed rest. The intervention most likely to be used for preventing blood clots for Joseph is

    a) TED hose.
    b) sequential stockings.
    c) massage therapy.
    d) anti-embolism stockings.

9.E   Choose the best response to the following scenarios.

1. Mrs. Dang had hip surgery four days ago. They have a doctor's order for TED stockings, which they are to wear at all times, except for skin care. Mrs. Dang is refusing to wear the stockings this morning, stating that they don't like them. What should you do?

    a) Ask them why they don't want to wear the TEDs, and then report to the nurse.
    b) Do not put the stockings on, since they have the right to refuse.
    c) Reapproach them the next morning.
    d) Instruct them on the dangers of blood clots after surgery.

2. Your resident tells you they want their bed linens changed every day, but the facility recommends changing bed linens only on bath day. What should you do?

    a) Change the bed only on bath day as per the facility policy.
    b) Report the request to the nurse so the resident's care plan can be updated.
    c) Tell the resident that you will change the bed daily, but do not do it.
    d) Compromise and change the bed three times a week.

3. One of your residents has had an incontinent episode while in bed. You gather clean linens and begin an occupied bed change when the resident's roommate enters the room. What should you do?

    a) Tell the roommate that they must remain in the hall until you say they may enter.
    b) Ignore the roommate and continue with the bed change.
    c) Ask the roommate if they would be able to wait in the hall until you are done.
    d) Turn on the call light and ask the nurse to change the linens for you.

4. Your resident has had five large loose bowel movements during your shift. What should you do?

    a) Only use hand sanitizer when caring for this resident.
    b) Obtain a stool specimen to check for possible illness.
    c) Return home to change your uniform.
    d) Report the loose stools to the nurse and follow their directives.

5. Your resident is having difficulty breathing and asks you to turn their oxygen up to 5 liters. What would you do?

    a) Promptly turn the oxygen up to 5 liters for them; this is their right.
    b) Report the shortness of breath to the nurse right away and ask that the nurse assess the resident.
    c) Report the shortness of breath to the nurse at the end of the shift.
    d) Ask the resident to turn it up themself, since this is out of your scope of practice.

6. You are removing soiled linens from a bed with your gloves on and realize you forgot to bring a clean top sheet. What should you do?

    a) Keep the gloves on and go get the top sheet.
    b) Put a pair of clean gloves over the dirty pair before getting the top sheet.
    c) Make the bed without the top sheet; you will remember to do that later.
    d) Remove your gloves, perform hand hygiene, and retrieve a top sheet.

7. Your resident who has a chronic lung disease is calling you into their room every 10 minutes for a variety of small tasks. What should you do?

    a) Explain to them that you do not have time to keep coming into their room.
    b) Only answer the call light every 30 minutes to allow time to care for others.
    c) Reassure the resident and update the nurse.
    d) Take the call light away from the resident while caring for your other residents' needs.

8. You care for a resident who is normally alert and oriented. Today they are confused. They are unable to tell you where they live or follow simple directives. What should you do?

    a) Update the nurse right away.
    b) Try reorientation therapy.
    c) Call the resident's family to update them.
    d) Obtain a urine sample.

9. You were asked to strain urine for a possible kidney stone. You forgot to strain and accidentally dumped the urine into the toilet. What should you do?

    a) Make sure to strain the resident's urine next time.
    b) Update the nurse and make sure to strain the next time.
    c) Omit this restroom trip from your documentation.
    d) Put a sign in the bathroom stating that the resident has a kidney stone.

10. You notice your resident taking off their nasal cannula and not wearing it as prescribed. What should you do?

    a) Ask them why they don't use it and then report this to the nurse.
    b) Turn off the oxygen so that it is not wasted.
    c) Tell them that they must wear the oxygen according to the doctor's orders.
    d) Turn down the oxygen's flow rate.

11. Your resident is applying Vaseline™ petroleum jelly to their nares due to dryness from oxygen use. What is the BEST response?

    a) Assist them in applying the jelly to prevent more nosebleeds.
    b) Take the petroleum jelly away and give it to the nurse.
    c) Report to the nurse and offer them a water-soluble lubricant.
    d) Tell them to stay away from fire or sparks.

12. You find an oxygen cylinder sitting upright in a resident's room. It is not being used. What should you do?

    a) Leave it there; the resident might have to use it later.
    b) Take it to the proper storage area.
    c) Lay it on its side so that it doesn't fall over.
    d) Place it in the resident's closet for safekeeping.

13. Your surgical resident is very tired but continuously has a room full of visitors who are making a lot of noise. What should you do?

    a) Do nothing; they have the right to visit.
    b) Ask the visitors to allow the resident to rest.
    c) Tell the visitors to go home and return later.
    d) Wait for them to leave, and then care for the resident.

14. Your resident had surgery yesterday and is doing well. The doctor has written the order to advance the diet as tolerated. They tell you they are starving and want to order a pizza. What should you do?

    a) Check their care plan to determine their current diet.
    b) Order them a pizza from the hospital kitchen.
    c) Encourage their family to bring a pizza to the facility for them.
    d) Tell them that they should remain on a liquid diet for 24 hours after surgery.

15. Your resident is on continuous oxygen. You find them sitting outside smoking a cigarette. What should you do?

    a) Remove all residents from that side of the building.
    b) Take the cigarettes and lighter away from them immediately.
    c) Immediately report this to the nurse.
    d) Tell them that they need to take cigarette breaks only when staff is with them.

16. You are caring for a resident who has been admitted to the long-term care facility for physical therapy following knee surgery. Their care plan states that they are weight-bearing as tolerated, but they refuse to ambulate with you. What should you do?

    a) Encourage the resident to walk small amounts.
    b) Tell the nurse that the resident is having pain.
    c) Ask the resident to do leg exercises in bed instead.
    d) Let the resident stay in bed since it is their right.

This page intentionally left blank.

Module 10: Vital Signs

10.A   Matching Definitions

_____ 1. Bradycardia

_____ 2. Lymphedema

_____ 3. Tachypnea

_____ 4. Bradypnea

_____ 5. Tachycardia

_____ 6. Korotkoff sound

_____ 7. Hypotension

_____ 8. Hypertension

A. Breathing that is too fast; respirations are greater than 20 breaths per minute

B. A low heart rate; less than 60 beats per minute

C. Blood pressure that is too low; typically any measurements lower than 90/60 mmHg

D. A high heart rate; greater than 100 beats per minute

E. Blood pressure that is too high; measurements are higher than 130/80 mmHg

F. Slow breathing; respirations are less than 12 breaths per minute

G. Heartbeats heard through the stethoscope while taking blood pressure

H. Painful swelling of the arm

10.B   Reflective Short-Answer Exercises

You work in a long-term care facility and are caring for Herman tonight. While you are walking with them, they become dizzy and fall. You alert the nurse immediately, and the nurse directs you to take Herman's vital signs. You report these to the nurse. Herman's temperature is 99.9°F, taken axillary, pulse is 108, respirations are 14, and blood pressure is 190/98.

1. Was it an appropriate time to take a set of vital signs on Herman? Why or why not?

_____

_____

_____

_____

2. What would you need to do with the vital sign equipment after using it on Herman?

_____

_____

_____

3. Was Herman's temperature normal? What is the normal range for an axillary temperature?

_____

_____

_____

_____

4. Was Herman's pulse within normal limits? What is the normal range for an adult's pulse?

_____
_____
_____
_____

5. Were Herman's respirations within normal limits? What is the normal range for respirations?

_____
_____
_____
_____

6. Was Herman's blood pressure within normal limits? What is the normal range for blood pressure?

_____
_____
_____
_____

7. Should the vital signs you obtained be documented? Why or why not?

_____
_____
_____
_____

10.C   Fill in the blanks using terms found in the word bank.

tachypnea	stethoscope	mastectomy
seconds	electronic cuff	equipment
sixty	hypertension	pediatric
admission	swelling	accurate
tachycardia	hours	hypotension
bradypnea	fever	non-contact infrared
pulse oximetry		

1. The nursing assistant must choose the correct cuff size when obtaining a resident's blood pressure. Sizes available typically include _____, adult, or extra-large.

2. You should never take a blood pressure reading on the arm of the same side of the body as a _____.

3. Bradycardia is a heart rate less than _____ beats per minute.

4. A set of vital signs is taken upon _____ to use as a baseline for the resident during their stay at the facility.

5. A heart rate of greater than 100 beats per minute is called _____.

6. A blood pressure reading less than 90/60 is called _____.

7. The Korotkoff sound is heartbeats heard via a _____ while taking blood pressure.

8. Blood pressure that is too high is called _____.

9. Wrist cuffs are small, convenient devices for taking a resident's blood pressure but often yield the least _____ reading.

10. If a resident is on infection control precautions or in isolation, a set of vital sign _____ should stay in the resident's room.

11. A _____ thermometer is the least invasive way to take a temperature.

12. _____ measures oxygen levels in the blood.

13. Breathing that is too fast and typically shallow is called _____.

14. _____ is slow breathing, less than 12 breaths per minute.

15. You can obtain a resident's blood pressure by using a stethoscope and sphygmomanometer or by using a(n) _____.

16. When using a temporal artery scanner, you should remove the resident's hat and wait for about 60 _____ before taking the temperature.

17. You typically will be taking a resident's vital signs each shift for 72 _____ following a fall.

18. A _____ means a person's temperature is above the normal range, typically greater than 100°F.

19. Lymphedema is a painful _____ of the arm.

10.D Multiple-Choice Exercises

1. The resident likely to have their vital signs taken MOST often would be a(n)

   a) 80-year-old resident who fell a week ago.
   b) 76-year-old resident admitted to the hospital with pneumonia.
   c) 24-year-old home health resident with Down syndrome.
   d) 82-year-old resident with dementia living in an assisted-living facility.

2. To find a radial pulse, you should find the natural groove of the resident's wrist using

   a) your index and middle fingers.
   b) your thumb.
   c) your index finger only.
   d) either your index finger or thumb.

3. You have a resident who is in contact isolation due to infection. A full set of vital sign equipment for the resident needs to be kept

   a) in the resident's room.
   b) right outside the resident's door.
   c) at the nurse's desk.
   d) in the dirty supply closet.

4. Weight is usually measured

   a) when a resident refuses a meal.
   b) once a year on the annual admission date.
   c) on the resident's bath day.
   d) at none of these times.

5. To prevent the spread of infection, vital sign equipment must be

   a) kept in all resident rooms.
   b) cleaned with alcohol after each use.
   c) used once and then discarded.
   d) cleaned with soap and water before each use.

6. When taking a resident's blood pressure, the cuff must be

   a) comfortable enough to fit around the arm without overlapping.
   b) loose enough to place two fingers under the cuff.
   c) tight enough to overlap slightly.
   d) both b and c.

7. The average temperature taken with a temporal artery scanner is

   a) 95.6°F.
   b) 97.6°F.
   c) 98.6°F.
   d) 99.6°F.

8. You are asked to get a temperature on a resident who has just finished eating their supper. Since you only have an oral thermometer available, you will need to wait

   a) 3 to 5 minutes.
   b) 5 to 10 minutes.
   c) 15 to 20 minutes.
   d) more than 20 minutes.

9. You are caring for a resident with advanced dementia. The nurse asks you to obtain the resident's temperature. The safest method for measuring this resident's temperature is

   a) oral.
   b) axillary.
   c) rectal.
   d) tympanic.

10. The average temperature taken with a tympanic thermometer is

    a) 98.6°F.
    b) 99.6°F.
    c) 96.6°F.
    d) 97.6°F.

11. The method that is least invasive and most accurate for obtaining a temperature is

    a) axillary.
    b) rectal.
    c) temporal.
    d) oral.

12. When placing a tympanic thermometer into an adult resident's ear, you should

    a) pull the ear back and slightly downward.
    b) pull the ear back and slightly upward.
    c) insert the thermometer without touching or pulling on the resident's ear.
    d) pull the ear either upward or downward, according to the resident's preference.

13. Which of the following pulse oximetry reading(s) will most likely require a respiratory intervention?

    a) 98%
    b) 93%
    c) 85%
    d) Both B and C

14. The least accurate method of measuring a resident's temperature is

    a) axillary.
    b) rectal.
    c) tympanic.
    d) oral.

15. Inaccurate results when using a tympanic thermometer may be due to

    a) buildup of earwax.
    b) user error.
    c) not obtaining a tight seal in the ear canal.
    d) all of the above.

10.E Choose the best response to the following scenarios.

1. Your resident's blood pressure is 240/230 after you take the blood pressure reading twice with the electronic blood pressure cuff. Your resident says they feel fine. What should you do?

   a) Report to the nurse and ask them to obtain a reading with a stethoscope and sphygmomanometer.

   b) Assume the electronic blood pressure cuff is correct and tell the nurse that the resident needs immediate care.

   c) Request that the nurse transport the resident to the emergency room immediately.

   d) Assume the electronic cuff is broken and report this to the nurse at the end of the shift.

2. You are trying to obtain a set of vital signs on one of your residents. They continue to talk while you are counting respirations. What should you do?

   a) Tell the nurse you are unable to obtain the respirations.

   b) Estimate the number of breaths in one minute.

   c) Wait patiently for the resident to finish speaking, then restart the count.

   d) Explain to the resident that you are trying to count their breaths.

3. Your nursing assistant training did not include instruction on how to properly take a blood pressure, and you are now required to do this. What should you do?

   a) Get your textbook and read the chapter on how to take a blood pressure.

   b) Politely inform the nurse that it is not within your scope of practice.

   c) Let the other nursing assistants take the blood pressure.

   d) Ask your immediate supervisor to take the blood pressure.

4. Your resident refuses to let you weigh them. What should you do?

   a) Report the resident's refusal to the nurse right away.

   b) Reassure them that you have obtained the weight of residents a lot larger than they are.

   c) Ask the nurse to get the resident's weight, as the nurse has a better relationship with the resident.

   d) Respect the resident's wishes and reattempt to obtain their weight the next morning.

5. Your task is to obtain vital signs on seven residents. You are going from room to room taking vital signs. You obtain the vital signs of your fifth resident and they are abnormal. What should you do?

   a) Continue to take the last two sets of vital signs and then report the abnormal findings to the nurse.

   b) After retaking the vital signs to confirm they are abnormal, report to the nurse right away and then continue to take the last two sets.

   c) Take the last two sets, and then report all the vital signs taken to the nurse at the end of the shift.

   d) Immediately report the abnormal vital signs to the nurse and then continue to take the last two sets.

6. You need to obtain a blood pressure for a resident who has an IV placed in their left arm. The resident states that they want their blood pressure taken in the left arm since they had surgery on their right arm many years ago. What should you do?

   a) Obtain the blood pressure using the resident's right arm.

   b) Ask the nurse to obtain the blood pressure.

   c) Request the nurse to stop the IV long enough to obtain the blood pressure.

   d) Check the resident's chart to verify whether you may use the right arm for obtaining the blood pressure.

This page intentionally left blank.

Module 11: Nutrition

11.A Matching Definitions

_____ 1. Enteral feeding

_____ 2. Hypervitaminosis

_____ 3. Blood glucose

_____ 4. Dehydration

_____ 5. Lactose

_____ 6. Lipids

_____ 7. Calorie

_____ 8. Lactase

_____ 9. Total parenteral nutrition (TPN)

_____ 10. Malnutrition

A. Fat molecules needed by the body to make use of fat-soluble vitamins; usually given along with TPN

B. A fluid filled with all the vitamins and minerals a person needs, usually including lipids

C. The enzyme that breaks down lactose

D. The energy the body needs to perform life functions within all its different cells; blood sugar

E. Occurs when the body takes in less fluid than it sends out; the body does not have adequate fluids to maintain normal body function

F. The sugar found in milk and some dairy products

G. A unit of measurement; measures food energy

H. A means by which nutrients in a special formula are transported directly into the stomach via a surgically implanted tube

I. Occurs when the body does not receive the nutrients or calories needed

J. A high level of vitamins in the body causing toxic symptoms

11.B Reflective Short-Answer Exercises

Oliver is one of your residents at the long-term care facility at which you work. They have diabetes with uncontrolled blood sugar levels. Oliver also has heart disease, high cholesterol, and open sores on their feet. They have refused their supper tray this evening, stating that they want to have pepperoni pizza and regular soda for supper. Oliver has called their family to ask them to bring pizza every Friday, since that is what they always did at home.

1. Is it Oliver's right to eat poorly? Why or why not?

_____

_____

_____

_____

2. How can you encourage Oliver to make healthy food choices?

_____

_____

_____

3. What actions should you take if Oliver continues to refuse the offered meal?

_____

_____

_____

4. What types of carbohydrates will Oliver be ingesting with their choice of supper?

_____

_____

_____

5. What types of fat do you think would be part of Oliver's chosen supper?

_____

_____

_____

6. How might eating these types of fat affect their health?

_____

_____

_____

7. What food would be a protein source in Oliver's chosen meal?

_____

_____

_____

8. Would this be a good protein source? Why or why not?

_____

_____

_____

9. What diet—or diets—might Oliver benefit from? Why?

_____

_____

_____

_____

11.C Fill in the blanks using terms found in the word bank.

dairy	fiber	hypervitaminosis
MyPyramid	vegetables	fat molecules
water-soluble	less	encourages
starches	enzyme	water
calories	dialysis	grains
muscle	malnutrition	MyPlate
blood sugar		

1. _____ has been phased out and replaced with MyPlate.

2. The human body is not able to break down _____, a type of complex carbohydrate.

3. _____ provides the energy our body needs to perform life functions within all its different cells.

4. A person taking too many fat-soluble vitamins can develop _____.

5. The basic forms of carbohydrates are sugars, _____, and fiber.

6. Lactase is the _____ that breaks down lactose.

7. Lactose is the sugar found in milk and some _____ products.

8. Lipids are the _____ needed by the body to make use of fat-soluble vitamins.

9. On average, adults should get about six to eight servings of _____ per day.

10. Amino acids are made into specialized proteins that make _____ and blood components.

11. Healthy eating _____ healthy lifestyles.

12. _____ is an online tool that can help you choose the right types and amounts of food to eat each day.

13. _____ makes up about 60% of the body.

14. _____ occurs when the body does not receive the nutrients or calories needed.

15. Sometimes residents receiving _____ treatments may have only ice chips in place of water.

16. Adults should get at least 2–3 cups of _____ each day.

17. A typical adult should consume about 1,800 to 2,000 _____ per day.

18. Dehydration occurs when the body takes in _____ fluid than it puts out.

19. There are two different types of vitamins: fat-soluble and _____.

11.D   Multiple-Choice Exercises

1. Dietary Guidelines for Americans suggests making half of your plate

    a) fruits and vegetables.
    b) whole grains.
    c) proteins.
    d) dairy.

2. MyPlate can assist you in making good food choices by helping to

    a) identify which foods should be increased.
    b) determine which foods should be decreased.
    c) focus on balancing calories.
    d) do all of the above.

3. A resident who is having difficulties at meal-times may be evaluated by the

    a) speech therapist.
    b) physical therapist.
    c) occupational therapist.
    d) both a and c.

4. Your resident drank one 8-ounce glass of milk and one 4-ounce glass of orange juice. The amount of fluid that needs to be documented is

    a) 12 cc.
    b) 240 cc.
    c) 360 cc.
    d) 30 cc.

5. Your resident is having a hard time using the utensils at mealtime due to swollen joints from arthritis. What should you do?

    a) Feed them their meals and snacks.
    b) Let them eat with their fingers.
    c) Place the food items in separate dishes.
    d) Provide the resident with large-handled flatware.

6. When calculating a resident's fluid intake, you need to include

    a) gelatin.
    b) Popsicles.
    c) ice cream.
    d) all of the above.

7. A good source of complex carbohydrates would be

    a) honey.
    b) pork chops.
    c) black beans.
    d) corn syrup.

8. The body uses calcium for

    a) reducing inflammation.
    b) bone growth.
    c) wound healing.
    d) vision health.

9. The recommended amount of grain for an average adult is

    a) 3–4 servings each day.
    b) 6–8 servings each day.
    c) 8–10 servings each day.
    d) none of the above.

10. You need to record the fluid intake of one of your residents. They drank 6 ounces of water, 8 ounces of milk, and 2 ounces of juice. The amount of fluid you should document is

    a) 160 cc.
    b) 320 cc.
    c) 420 cc.
    d) 480 cc.

11. Your responsibilities when caring for a resident with diabetes include

    a) ensuring that the nurse has checked the resident's blood sugar before meals.
    b) informing the resident that they must follow their diabetic diet.
    c) teaching the resident what foods are included in a diabetic diet.
    d) telling their family not to bring home-cooked foods to the resident.

12. A resident with celiac disease should avoid eating

    a) most grains.
    b) fruits and vegetables.
    c) dairy products.
    d) meats high in fat.

13. The lunch menu for today includes split pea soup. What food group does the soup belong to?

    a) proteins
    b) vegetables
    c) grains
    d) both a and b

14. A resident who is on a low-sodium diet should avoid eating

    a) brown rice.
    b) oatmeal.
    c) cottage cheese.
    d) spinach.

15. You are assisting a resident who has difficulty drinking their fluids due to limited neck movement. The BEST assistive device for them to use during meals would be a

    a) spout cup.
    b) nonskid mat.
    c) nosey cup.
    d) small, rubber-tipped spoon.

16. Before meals, you should make sure all residents have

    a) clean hands.
    b) a clothing protector on.
    c) their food cut up.
    d) salt and pepper to season their food.

17. Lawrence is an older resident with Parkinson's disease. They find it hard to feed themself due to shaky hands. The adaptive device that would MOST increase their independence during mealtimes is a

    a) straw.
    b) covered cup.
    c) nonskid mat.
    d) plate guard.

18. Amanda is a 60-year-old resident recovering from a recent car accident. They have a broken right arm and hand. An appropriate diet for them might be a(n)

    a) pureed diet.
    b) enteral feeding.
    c) cut-up diet.
    d) ground diet.

19. Micah is on a lactose-free diet. Today's lunch menu includes ice cream for dessert. The person responsible for ensuring that Micah is not accidentally served ice cream is the

    a) nurse.
    b) nursing assistant.
    c) dietician.
    d) doctor.

20. Dehydration can be a result of

    a) nausea and vomiting.
    b) diarrhea.
    c) poor fluid intake.
    d) all of the above.

21. You discover that one of your residents with diabetes has been keeping chocolate candy in their room. You should

    a) take the candy out of the room.
    b) inform the resident that they should not eat candy.
    c) leave the candy where you found it and update the nurse.
    d) replace the chocolate with sugar-free candy.

11.E   Choose the best response to the following scenarios.

1. Your resident has chosen to eat their breakfast in their room. You have their breakfast tray and are about to place it on the bedside table when you notice a full urinal on the table. What should you do?

    a) Place the food tray next to the full urinal and then empty the urinal.
    b) Empty the urinal, sanitize the bedside table, and then place their food on the bedside table.
    c) Place the urinal on top of the dresser next to them and then place their food on the bedside table.
    d) Ask the resident to eat in the dining room while you tidy their bedroom.

2. Your resident receives a mechanically altered diet and asks you what the green food is. What should you do?

    a) Tell them that you have no idea.
    b) Taste the food and offer an idea.
    c) Smell the food and offer an idea.
    d) Look at the day's menu and update the resident.

3. Alma is an older resident with dementia. You notice that they eat more at mealtime when they can pick things up with their fingers. What should you do?

    a) Continue to try and persuade them to eat with the utensils.
    b) Make sure they are wearing a clothing protector around their neck at all times.
    c) Update the nurse and ask if finger foods can be incorporated into their meals.
    d) Make sure that they have soft foods for every meal.

4. One of your residents refuses to follow a well-balanced diet and keeps many unhealthy snacks in their room. What should you do?

    a) Take the snacks away when they are napping.
    b) Tell the family to remove the snacks and not to bring more.
    c) Remove the snacks and then place them at the nurse's station.
    d) Update the nurse so that the nurse can reinforce diet recommendations with the resident.

5. Your resident is on a fluid restriction and asks you to fill their water pitcher above the allowed amount. What should you do?

    a) Fill the pitcher as the resident has requested.
    b) Fill the water pitcher with more ice.
    c) Remind the resident of their fluid restriction and update the nurse.
    d) Refuse to give them the requested amount.

6. Your resident vomits during dinner. What should you do?

    a) Clean the resident and then ask if they would like to eat the rest of their meal in their room.
    b) Take the resident to their room where you can care for them and then update the nurse.
    c) Offer another food choice like chicken noodle soup or gelatin.
    d) Clean the resident and then take them to their room for a nap.

7. You find your resident taking multiple vitamins brought from home while eating their breakfast. What should you do?

    a) Update the nurse right away.
    b) Ask the resident to give the vitamins to you.
    c) Tell the family that they need to take the vitamins home.
    d) Offer to put the vitamins in the locked drawer of the resident's bedside table.

8. While feeding one of your residents with dementia, they become agitated and spit food in your hair. What should you do?

   a) Firmly tell them that it is wrong to spit foods.
   b) Excuse yourself, clean up, and report the behavior to the nurse.
   c) Refuse to feed them the rest of the meal.
   d) Laugh it off; they don't know what they're doing.

This page intentionally left blank.

Module 12: Emergency Procedures

12.A Matching Definitions

_____ 1. Superficial burn

_____ 2. Full-thickness burn

_____ 3. Complete airway obstruction

_____ 4. Hypovolemic shock

_____ 5. Status epilepticus

_____ 6. Partial-thickness burn

_____ 7. Partial airway obstruction

_____ 8. Ambulatory

_____ 9. Anaphylactic shock

_____ 10. Gait

_____ 11. Syncope

_____ 12. Cardiac arrest

_____ 13. Cardiogenic shock

_____ 14. Restraint

_____ 15. Dangling

_____ 16. Hemorrhage

_____ 17. Aura

_____ 18. Seizure

A. Fainting; a sudden, temporary loss of consciousness

B. A life-threatening generalized seizure that lasts longer than 5 minutes

C. Uncontrollable dilation of all the blood vessels, usually from an allergic reaction

D. Disrupted electrical activity within the brain

E. Inability of the heart to pump enough blood to the body organs due to damage to the heart

F. Type of burn that involves the epidermis, dermis, and subcutaneous tissue; may also affect deep muscles and tendons

G. Type of burn that involves only the top layer of skin, the epidermis

H. Having the ability to walk about

I. A feeling or a visual disturbance experienced prior to a seizure

J. Type of burn that involves the epidermis and dermis

K. Any physical or chemical limitation to prevent or limit the resident from moving freely about their environment

L. Blood and fluid loss so extreme that the heart is unable to pump enough blood to support the body

M. Blockage of the airway that still allows for some air exchange

N. Excessive loss of blood, either internal or external

O. The heart cannot contract and pump blood; usually a result of heart attack or trauma

P. Sitting on the side of the bed after moving from a lying position; allows time for blood pressure to stabilize

Q. Very little to no air exchange due to blockage of the airway

R. A person's pattern of walking

12.B Reflective Short-Answer Exercises

Scenario 1:
You are assisting residents in the common dining room during mealtime. Damon, one of your residents, starts coughing violently. They stand up and start walking to their room. By the time they get to their room, you hear their cough getting weaker. As you approach, they shake their head no, indicating that they do not want your help. You notice that their face has become red, and they have a high-pitched wheeze.

1. Why would Damon walk away during a potentially life-threatening situation?

_____

_____

_____

_____

2. Should you give them privacy? Why or why not?

_____

_____

_____

_____

3. Should you attempt to start abdominal thrusts when they first start coughing? Why or why not?

_____

_____

_____

_____

4. Did Damon originally have a partial or complete obstruction?

_____

_____

_____

_____

5. What are the signs of a partial obstruction?

_____

_____

_____

_____

6. What type of obstruction did they ultimately have?

_____

_____

_____

_____

7. What are the signs of a complete obstruction?

_____

_____

_____

_____

8. When should you have activated EMS?

_____

_____

_____

_____

Scenario 2:

Sally is an 84-year-old woman who lives at home alone. One night while going to the bathroom, they tripped on a throw rug and fell. Sally was unable to get up on their own, and they lay on the floor until their daughter came to visit the next day. Sally's fall resulted in a broken hip and arm. After staying in the hospital for 3 nights, Sally is transferred to a nursing home for rehabilitation services.

1. What emotions do you think Sally will experience while in the hospital and nursing home?

_____

_____

_____

_____

2. What steps can the nursing assistant take to help Sally while they are in the nursing home?

_____

_____

_____

_____

3. What factors do you think could have contributed to Sally's fall?

_____

_____

_____

_____

4. What steps could have been taken to prevent Sally from falling?

_____

_____

_____

_____

Scenario 3:
Gerry suffers from dementia. When you take them to the bathroom or attempt to bathe them, they become very aggressive. They spit, pinch, and shout obscenities. Tonight, when you are getting them ready for bed, they punch you in the face, causing a black eye.

1. Will restraining Gerry decrease their aggressive behaviors? Why or why not?

    _____

    _____

    _____

    _____

2. What risks are there for Gerry if they are restrained?

    _____

    _____

    _____

    _____

3. Do you think giving Gerry a medication for their aggression might help? Why or why not?

    _____

    _____

    _____

    _____

4. What are the risks of starting an anti-anxiety or antipsychotic medication?

    _____

    _____

    _____

    _____

5. What are some alternative ways you could reduce Gerry's aggressive behavior instead of restraining them?

    _____

    _____

    _____

    _____

12.C   Fill in the blanks using terms found in the word bank.

abdominal thrusts	bed frame	programs
alarm systems	epidermis	range-of-motion
brain	emotional	function
2 hours	safety	chemical
Medicare	strengthening	core
quick-release	physical	Medicaid
balance	numbness	upright
15 minutes	Defibrillators/AEDs	

1. Perform _____ exercises on the bed-bound resident when the restraint is removed.

2. The Centers for _____ & _____ Services have rules to make sure that residents can freely move about their environment.

3. There are many different _____ and initiatives to help prevent falls.

4. A full-thickness burn is a type of burn that involves the _____, dermis, and subcutaneous tissue.

5. Every _____, the restraint must be removed.

6. The nursing assistant must check the skin under the restraint for warmth, pain, color, and _____.

7. A _____ restraint is an anti-anxiety or antipsychotic drug.

8. All restraints must be fastened with a _____ knot.

9. Never hold a resident _____ during a fall; you can injure yourself and the resident.

10. One symptom of distress could be a feeling of _____ or tingling in the face, lips, or extremities.

11. Balance retraining and _____ exercises can help reduce the risk of falls.

12. _____ are commonly found in public areas, such as schools.

13. A seizure is caused by disrupted electrical activity within the _____.

14. Tai chi is an example of light exercise that can strengthen _____ muscles, which aids in better _____.

15. The only appropriate reason to use a restraint is to ensure _____ of the resident and those around them.

16. If a restraint is used, the resident must be checked every _____.

17. A restraint must be secured to the _____.

18. _____ are sometimes referred to as the Heimlich maneuver.

19. Some facilities use _____ for residents who are at risk of falling.

20. The use of restraints can increase the risk of _____ and _____ harm.

12.D Multiple-Choice Exercises

1. Some facilities have taken side rails off all the residents' beds because

   a) residents may get their arms or legs caught.
   b) residents are at risk of strangling themselves.
   c) positioning devices are available and are not restraints.
   d) all of the above.

2. The use of restraints may lead to any of the following EXCEPT

   a) pressure injuries.
   b) decreased agitation.
   c) emotional upset.
   d) muscle weakness.

3. You are walking with Alma using a gait belt and pulling a wheelchair behind them. They suddenly become shaky and weak. They say that they see "dark spots." The FIRST thing you should do is

   a) get them some water or juice to drink.
   b) have them sit down in the wheelchair.
   c) report their symptoms to the nurse.
   d) take them outside for fresh air.

4. A resident experiencing a grand mal seizure

   a) has a weak pulse and low blood pressure.
   b) has chest pain and grayish skin.
   c) looks like they are staring off into space.
   d) collapses and shakes uncontrollably.

5. High-pitched wheezing is one sign of a

   a) complete airway obstruction.
   b) syncopal episode.
   c) partial airway obstruction.
   d) grand mal seizure.

6. You are assisting residents with their lunch when you notice that one of the residents takes a large bite of potatoes. They start coughing. You should

   a) ask them if they are choking and then do abdominal thrusts.
   b) have them take a drink of water.
   c) remain close and allow them to cough.
   d) ask them to raise their arms into the air.

7. The use of restraints can

   a) keep a resident safe from falls.
   b) prevent physical outbursts.
   c) decrease aggressive behavior.
   d) cause depression.

8. One example of a fall prevention strategy would be

   a) encouraging a resident to attend activities.
   b) having a resident lie in bed as much as possible.
   c) keeping a resident's wheelchair locked while they are in their room.
   d) placing an alarm on a resident's wheelchair.

9. Dangling means that before assisting a resident to stand, you

   a) make sure that the resident has their shoes and socks on.
   b) make sure that the resident's feet are flat on the floor.
   c) allow time for the blood pressure to stabilize.
   d) allow the resident's feet to swing freely while sitting.

10. You discover one of your residents with dementia in the housekeeping closet. They have redness around their mouth. The FIRST step you should take is to

    a) find out what they ate or drank.
    b) activate EMS.
    c) contact the poison center.
    d) rinse their mouth with water.

11. A resident has accidentally spilled bathroom cleaner on their skin. To find information about this chemical, a nursing assistant should

    a) contact the emergency room.
    b) call the resident's doctor.
    c) look it up in the SDS.
    d) look it up on Wikipedia.

12. After a witnessed fall, the nurse is likely to ask you to obtain vital signs

    a) once each shift for the next 24 hours.
    b) once each shift for the next week.
    c) at the time of the fall only.
    d) once each shift for the next 72 hours.

13. You are assisting a resident who has burned themself. After activating EMS, your NEXT step is to

    a) cover the burn with a cool, moist sterile dressing.
    b) cover the burn with a dry sterile dressing.
    c) put a burn ointment on the wound.
    d) take vital signs and document the incident.

14. One of your residents has a wrist restraint. You should check the hand, fingers, and the area under the restraint every

   a) 2 hours.
   b) 15 minutes.
   c) hour.
   d) 30 minutes.

15. The type of shock caused by extreme blood loss is called

   a) hypovolemic.
   b) syncopal.
   c) cardiogenic.
   d) anaphylactic.

16. Signs of shock include all of the following EXCEPT

   a) cool and clammy skin.
   b) a weak pulse.
   c) a drop in blood pressure.
   d) decreased respiratory rate.

17. You enter a resident's room to find them lying on the floor. They are bleeding from a large cut across their forehead. The FIRST thing you should do is

   a) put on a pair of gloves.
   b) activate EMS.
   c) apply sterile dressings to the forehead.
   d) assist them to a recovery position.

18. Grace is an 80-year-old resident who has had two recent falls. You notice that you need to tell them to look up when they are walking. They look down at their feet instead. This is likely because they are

   a) not listening to you.
   b) afraid of falling again.
   c) not able to follow directions.
   d) not steady enough to walk.

19. Once cardiopulmonary resuscitation (CPR) is started, it can only be stopped if

   a) you are no longer able to feel a pulse.
   b) the ambulance driver declares the resident dead.
   c) someone qualified takes over.
   d) it has been longer than 6 minutes since it was started.

20. Doris is a resident who has fallen and has a gash across their left arm. You apply pressure to the wound using a sterile dressing. The dressing is soaked through, and the bleeding is not slowing. Your next step should be to

   a) remove the soaked dressing before applying a new dressing to the wound.
   b) place another dressing on top of the soiled dressing and apply pressure to the artery above the wound.
   c) apply a tourniquet above the gash to stop the bleeding from the wound.
   d) place Doris in the recovery position and elevate their legs to increase circulation to the heart.

21. All of the following put a resident at risk of falling EXCEPT

   a) buildup of earwax.
   b) frequent naps.
   c) antidepressant medications.
   d) walking without shoes.

22. When a resident is having a seizure, the nursing assistant should

   a) hold the resident in place so they don't hit anything.
   b) place a spoon in their mouth to prevent swallowing the tongue.
   c) note what time the seizure starts and ends.
   d) activate EMS if the seizure lasts longer than one minute.

23. Elena often gets out of bed to walk to the bathroom. Yesterday they tripped on their bedside table and fell. An appropriate fall prevention strategy would be to

   a) post a sign reminding them to ask for help.
   b) have them go to bed earlier so they are more alert.
   c) place a soft mat on the floor next to their bed.
   d) place an alarm on their bed.

24. Wilson recently had surgery on their hip. They have asked you to put their side rails up to make it easier for them to move in bed. You should

    a) put the side rails up, since Wilson is using them for positioning.
    b) tell Wilson that side rails are a restraint and shouldn't be used.
    c) put the side rails up after the nurse gets informed consent.
    d) instruct Wilson on side rail risks and then put them up.

25. The person MOST at risk of falling would be a

    a) 30-year-old woman who had gallbladder surgery.
    b) 77-year-old man living at home and on pain medications.
    c) 21-year-old woman who takes medication for depression.
    d) 67-year-old woman with a history of asthma.

26. Dennis is an older resident at risk of falling because they forget to lock their wheelchair brakes before standing. The BEST way to prevent Dennis from falling is to

    a) tell them that they are not allowed to stand by themself.
    b) place them by the nurse's desk with the wheels locked.
    c) put leg rests on the wheelchair to keep them from standing.
    d) have anti-rollback brakes placed on their wheelchair.

27. One of your residents has restraints on their ankles. You should alert the nurse right away if

    a) they complain that their foot feels numb.
    b) their foot feels warm when you touch it.
    c) they do foot exercises without your assistance.
    d) they need their incontinence product changed.

28. Elsa is an older resident who has a lot of anxiety and easily becomes upset. The doctor orders medication to help with their anxiety. Today Elsa had to be assisted with their lunch because they were very drowsy. This is an example of

    a) a chemical restraint.
    b) an environmental restraint.
    c) a normal part of aging.
    d) negligence.

29. A nursing assistant can help prevent the use of restraints by

    a) placing an alarm on residents' wheelchairs.
    b) keeping residents on routine schedules.
    c) telling residents' families that they need to visit daily.
    d) using side rails to keep residents in bed.

30. You are ambulating a resident using a gait belt and a walker. They suddenly become weak and begin to fall. You should

    a) try to catch them before they fall to the floor.
    b) have them lean on the walker until they are rested and steady.
    c) lower them to the floor using the gait belt and both hands.
    d) lower them to the floor with one hand on the gait belt.

31. David has fallen in their room. The nurse directs you to assist them to their bed, but they are too weak to help with the transfer. You should

    a) use a gait belt and an assist of two to help them to their feet.
    b) put a sheet under them and ask a coworker to help lift them.
    c) allow them to rest and to regain their strength before moving them.
    d) use a mechanical lift to move them to their bed.

32. The FIRST step in preventing falls is

    a) assisting residents with their basic needs.
    b) providing exercise classes.
    c) placing alarms on wheelchairs and beds as needed.
    d) identifying who is at risk of a fall.

12.E Choose the best response to the following scenarios.

1. You are ambulating your resident, and they have a syncopal episode. What is the FIRST action you should take?

   a) Put them in a reclining chair with their feet elevated.
   b) Help them to the floor while protecting their head.
   c) Take them to the restroom after the episode.
   d) Apply an ice pack to their forehead for 20 minutes.

2. You are sitting at the breakfast table with a resident who collapses and begins to shake uncontrollably. What should you do?

   a) Clear the room.
   b) Send your coworker for an ice pack.
   c) Note the time and keep the resident safe.
   d) Do all of the above.

3. One of your residents is coughing and obviously choking. What should you do?

   a) Start chest compressions.
   b) Call 911.
   c) Stand by and wait to help if needed.
   d) Offer a drink of water.

4. You find your resident on the floor with no pulse. The resident has expressed in the past that they do not want to be resuscitated. What should you do?

   a) Yell for help and start CPR.
   b) Activate EMS.
   c) Put the call light on.
   d) Call the resident's doctor.

5. Your home care resident is at risk for falls due to several throw rugs in their path. What should you do?

   a) Remove the rugs and place them in a closet.
   b) Remind the resident that the rugs pose a danger and then report to your supervisor.
   c) Buy rugs with nonskid grip for the resident.
   d) Call the resident's daughter and ask the daughter to remove the rugs.

6. One of your residents may have ingested some household cleaner. What should you do?

   a) Report to the supervisor immediately.
   b) Give them a glass of water or milk.
   c) Make them vomit.
   d) Observe them for changes and then update the doctor.

7. You witness a resident fall in their bedroom. What should you do?

   a) Assist the resident back to their feet.
   b) Check the resident for injuries and then update the nurse.
   c) Help the resident into bed and then alert the nurse.
   d) Stay with the resident and call out for the nurse.

8. You notice one of your residents with dementia crawling around on the floor of their room. What should you do?

   a) Ask the nurse to give the resident medication to calm them.
   b) Politely tell the resident to stop being so disruptive.
   c) Put the resident back in bed and tell them to remain there.
   d) Make sure the resident is safe and try to redirect them.

9. While you are ambulating a resident, they state that they are dizzy. What should you do?

    a) Assist the resident to a sitting position.
    b) Keep going until the dizziness passes.
    c) Allow them to stand and regain their strength.
    d) Tighten your grip on the transfer belt while they continue to walk.

10. The nurse has obtained a doctor's order for wrist restraints and asks you to apply them to a confused resident. What is your best response?

    a) Place the wrist restraints on the resident as directed.
    b) Tell the nurse that wrist restraints should never be used for residents.
    c) Tell the nurse that they will need to apply the restraint the first time, and then you can assist afterward.
    d) Tell the nurse that you feel a chemical restraint would be more appropriate.

11. Your resident continues to unfasten their waist restraint and stand up out of their chair. What should you do?

    a) Make sure the restraint is tied in a knot.
    b) Call the resident's doctor for new instructions.
    c) Take the restraint off.
    d) Update your supervisor.

12. An older, confused resident is yelling and disrupting the other residents in the dining area. What should you do?

    a) Take them to their room and shut the door.
    b) Try to anticipate what they may need.
    c) Tell them to sit down and be respectful of others.
    d) Move the other residents away from them.

13. Your resident continues to wander into other residents' rooms with their wheelchair. What should you do?

    a) Lock their wheelchair so that they cannot roam.
    b) Put them in a recliner with the legs up.
    c) Invite them to go for a walk with you.
    d) Put them in front of the television.

14. Your resident asks you to raise the side rail of the bed before leaving the room. What should you do?

    a) Raise the side rail for them; residents have the right to make their own decisions.
    b) Refuse to raise the side rail and instruct them on the risks of using side rails.
    c) Raise both rails and make sure the bed is in the low position.
    d) Tell your supervisor that the resident is asking for side rails.

Module 13: Long-Term Care Patient

13.A   Matching Definitions

Sections A–B

_____ 1. Dementia

_____ 2. Elopement

_____ 3. Melanocyte

_____ 4. Dermis

_____ 5. Subcutaneous layer

_____ 6. Tissue

_____ 7. Epidermis

_____ 8. Epithelial tissue

_____ 9. Integumentary system

_____ 10. Alimentary canal

_____ 11. Smooth muscle

_____ 12. Nervous tissue

_____ 13. Peristalsis

_____ 14. Skeletal muscle

_____ 15. Sundowning

_____ 16. Cell

_____ 17. Organ

_____ 18. Hormone

_____ 19. Muscle tissue

_____ 20. Organ system

_____ 21. Peripheral nerves

_____ 22. Connective tissue

_____ 23. Dysphagia

_____ 24. Cardiac muscle

A. The same type of cells grouped together; the four types of cells are epithelial, connective, muscle, and nervous

B. The nerves that transmit signals to and from the spinal cord, allowing communication among the brain, the spinal cord, and the rest of the body

C. The middle layer of skin

D. A chemical that is secreted within the body by one of the endocrine glands, by certain organs of the body, or by adipose tissue

E. The skin, hair, sweat glands, fingernails, and toenails

F. A cell in the skin that produces melanin, which gives color to the skin

G. Tissue that makes movement by contracting and relaxing when stimulated; the three types include smooth, cardiac, and skeletal

H. When one organ functions in cooperation with another organ

I. Tissue that sends, transmits, and receives electrical impulses, or messages, between the body and the brain

J. Muscle tissue that contracts and relaxes involuntarily

K. A type of tissue that forms a matrix between the cells; it includes blood, bone, cartilage, and fat

L. The outermost layer of skin

M. A specialized type of muscle tissue that forms the heart and, when stimulated, forces it to beat involuntarily

N. Skin tissue that lines our bodies inside and out

O. A cognitively challenged resident leaving the protection of a home or facility unsupervised

definitions continued on next page

P. The passage that makes up the digestive system, consisting of the mouth, pharynx, esophagus, stomach, small intestine, large intestine, rectum, and anus

Q. The involuntary action of smooth muscle contracting and relaxing rhythmically

R. Tissue type found wherever there are moving parts of the body; movement is voluntary and purposeful

S. An increase in agitation and restlessness occurring later in the day and into the evening

T. Two or more tissue types that function together

U. The smallest living unit of the body

V. Difficulty swallowing

W. The deepest layer of skin, where adipose tissue is found

X. A general term describing loss of memory and brain function

Sections C–E

_____ 1. Nonpharmacological pain management

_____ 2. Quality of life

_____ 3. Holistic care

_____ 4. Homeostasis

_____ 5. Self-actualization

_____ 6. Esteem

A. A measure of happiness regarding physical comfort, emotional health, spiritual wellness, and social activity

B. Care that ensures that physical, emotional, and spiritual needs are addressed when caring for the resident

C. Managing pain without the use of drugs

D. Meeting one's own social, creative, emotional, and spiritual needs

E. Respect or admiration

F. State in which internal body processes remain stable despite external variables

Section F

1. Fomite
2. Kyphosis
3. Palliative care
4. Stasis ulcer
5. Orthopnea
6. Arrhythmia
7. Cystocele
8. Aspiration
9. Kaposi's sarcoma
10. Pressure injury
11. Benign tumor
12. Atrophy
13. Diaphoresis
14. Angina
15. Metastasis
16. Hallucination
17. Carcinogens
18. Peripheral lower extremity edema
19. Dyspnea
20. HIV
21. Delusion
22. Malignant tumor
23. Dysrhythmia
24. Contracture
25. Cancer
26. Modifiable risk factors
27. AIDS
28. Nocturia
29. Nonmodifiable risk factors

A. A term used for diseases in which abnormal cells divide without control and are able to invade other tissues

B. Shortness of breath

C. A physical shortening of the joint ligaments

D. A cancer caused by a virus that is closely related to AIDS infections

E. An ulcer that results from poor blood flow to the lower extremities; often seen in peripheral vascular disease

F. A gradual loss, or wasting, of muscle mass

G. A tumor that is cancerous

H. Excessive sweating

I. The perception of a smell, sight, sound, taste, or sensation that is not really there

J. Painful swelling of the legs and feet

K. Lifestyle choices that an individual has control over

L. Characteristics of oneself that cannot change

M. An irregular heartbeat; also known as a dysrhythmia

N. A prolapsed bladder

O. The inability to lie flat due to excess fluid retention; most often occurs with congestive heart failure

P. Inhaling vomit, food, or saliva into the lungs

Q. End stage of an HIV infection

R. Substances that are known to cause cancer

S. An inanimate object that harbors a germ or parasite

T. The need to urinate frequently through the night

U. Cancer that has spread or moved to other areas of the body

V. Occurs when pressure over a bony prominence is not relieved and the blood supply to that area is cut off

W. A tumor that is not cancerous

definitions continued on next page

X. A belief in something that is not true or not supported by evidence

Y. Interventions that help relieve the resident's pain and stress related to any serious medical issue

Z. The forward bending of the upper back, giving the classic hunched look of osteoporosis

AA. An irregular heartbeat, sometimes known as an arrhythmia

BB. Chest pain

CC. Human immunodeficiency virus

13.B   Reflective Short-Answer Exercises

Scenario 1

Paulo is an 83-year-old living at home alone. They take four different medications for diabetes, heart disease, and high cholesterol. They frequently get up at night to urinate. Paulo uses a small nightlight in the bathroom to help them see in the dark. Last night on the way to the bathroom, they fell. They were unable to get up off the floor on their own due to pain in their right hip. They remained on the floor until their daughter came to check on them the next morning.

1.   What injury could Paulo have due to their fall?

_____

_____

_____

_____

2.   Why would they be unable to get up from the floor?

_____

_____

_____

_____

3.   Which of Paulo's aging sensory organs could have been a factor in their fall? How?

_____

_____

_____

_____

4.   Could Paulo's medications have been a factor in their fall? If so, why?

_____

_____

_____

_____

5. Which of Paulo's body systems have likely been affected by age, and how could these changes have led to their fall?

_____
_____
_____
_____

Scenario 2

Frank is a 67-year-old man who normally requires light assistance with showers and dressing. They are a talkative and active resident. They are independent in their transfers and ambulation. Today when you enter their room, they are still in bed, which is unusual for them. Their face appears to droop on one side. When you help them out of bed, you notice that their left side is weak. They need a lot of assistance to transfer into a wheelchair. When you ask Frank if they are feeling well today, they seem confused and doesn't answer.

1. What do you think Frank may be experiencing?

_____
_____
_____
_____

2. Which of Frank's specific symptoms support your thoughts?

_____
_____
_____
_____

3. What other signs and symptoms might you see with this medical condition?

_____
_____
_____
_____

4. What do you think might happen to Frank if you were not familiar with the signs and symptoms of different medical conditions and your role in helping them as a nursing assistant?

_____
_____
_____
_____

Scenario 3

You are working in a long-term care facility. You care for Gene, who has dementia and does not talk to the staff or the other residents. They are sitting next to the nurse's station, waiting for their wife to come. You notice that they look upset. When you ask them if something is wrong, they just shake their head and look away from you.

1. List some examples of how you might be able to help Gene meet each level of Maslow's hierarchy of needs.

   _____

   _____

   _____

   _____

2. What developmental stage do you think Gene might be in? Why?

   _____

   _____

   _____

   _____

3. How can you best care for Gene?

   _____

   _____

   _____

   _____

4. How will you know if your interventions work or not? What signs would you see?

   _____

   _____

   _____

   _____

5. How could you positively affect Gene's quality of life?

   _____

   _____

   _____

   _____

6. How can you care for Gene holistically? List specific interventions that can help them meet their emotional, physical, and spiritual needs.

   _____

   _____

   _____

   _____

7. What kind of social activities could Gene participate in if they are not verbal?

_____
_____
_____
_____

8. How could you meet the needs of Gene's wife when they visit?

_____
_____
_____
_____

13.C   Fill in the blanks using terms found in the word bank.

modifiable	milestones	managed
unmet	plaques	healthy
behaviors	autopsy	memories
enhances	tangles	inactivity
individualized	obsessed	contagious
biopsy	genetics	sexual
chemotherapy	hunched	mental illness
sleep hygiene	central pump	

1. If the resident with cancer receives _____, the risk of infection increases because it limits the body's ability to make new white blood cells.

2. Kyphosis gives a person the classic _____ look of osteoporosis.

3. Alzheimer's disease is characterized by _____ and _____ that form in the brain.

4. Tending to the comfort of your resident _____ their quality of life.

5. Certain _____, such as impaired communication, wandering, and difficulty performing activities of daily living, are commonly seen in people with dementia.

6. Reminiscence therapy is used to help the resident recall distant _____ of their life.

7. The behaviors associated with dementia can be _____ by going through a checklist of common triggers or unmet needs.

8. High blood pressure and smoking are examples of _____ risk factors.

9. Cancers that have a _____ component include breast, colon, and some childhood cancers.

10. Even though some cancers are linked with infections, they are not _____. You cannot catch cancer from someone else.

11. A _____ is the removal of a small number of cells from a questionable area to test for cancer.

12. A cancer treatment plan must be _____ and may be based on how the tumor is reacting to the treatment.

13. Residents may display behaviors associated with dementia because of a(n) _____ need.

14. _____ inappropriateness may occur in the later stages of dementia, which can be quite upsetting to both the resident's family and others residing in the facility.

15. Maintaining a regular bedtime routine and providing quiet time before bed are ways to promote good _____ practices.

16. Choosing a _____ lifestyle, including eating healthy and getting regular exercise, can reduce your chances of developing dementia.

17. Normal human development is measured based on when a person achieves certain _____ at a given point in their life.

18. Residents with dementia may become _____ with leaving a facility to get home, and it is difficult to redirect them.

19. A diagnosis of Alzheimer's can only be confirmed upon _____.

20. _____ is a broad category of conditions that impact mood as well as how a person thinks, behaves, expresses emotions, and feels.

21. The lymphatic system is made of hollow vessels throughout the body to carry fluids but lacks a _____.

22. Physical _____ and poor diet are lifestyle choices that increase the risk of some types of cancer.

13.D Multiple-Choice Exercises

1. The social, creative, emotional, and spiritual potential in a person is called
   a) self-realization.
   b) self-image.
   c) self-actualization.
   d) self-esteem.

2. Epithelial tissue forms the
   a) brain and spinal cord.
   b) heart and muscle fibers.
   c) lining of the stomach and lungs.
   d) blood and bones of the skeleton.

3. The typical age when a child develops a sense of identity through experimentation is
   a) 2–3 years old.
   b) 4–5 years old.
   c) 6–11 years old.
   d) 12–19 years old.

4. Encouraging resident participation in a tour of a local art exhibit helps residents to meet their need for
   a) esteem.
   b) love and belonging.
   c) comfort.
   d) self-actualization.

5. The FIRST step in helping a resident who is emotionally unwell is to
   a) ensure that they are toileted promptly.
   b) offer them a chance to paint or put together puzzles.
   c) make sure that they don't wander into unsafe areas.
   d) encourage them to participate in activities.

6. Luther recently lost their job after working in a local factory for several years. They are having a difficult time supporting their family and themself. According to Maslow, the level of need they will meet when they find new employment is

   a) esteem.
   b) safety and security.
   c) love and belonging.
   d) basic human needs.

7. You are taking care of Molly and notice that their chart states that they are Catholic. Molly is resting, but you realize that your facility has Catholic services being held in the chapel. You should

   a) get Molly ready for church.
   b) let Molly continue resting.
   c) ask Molly if they would like to attend church.
   d) wait and take Molly to the next service.

8. Providing holistic care means paying attention to

   a) the resident's physical and emotional needs.
   b) the resident's social and spiritual needs.
   c) the resident's illness and level of function.
   d) both a and b.

9. One specific defense mechanism the body uses to protect itself is

   a) the lining of the lungs and trachea.
   b) white blood cells.
   c) the integumentary system.
   d) the lining of the sensory organs.

10. Blood, cartilage, fat, and bone are all made of

    a) nervous tissue.
    b) muscle tissue.
    c) epithelial tissue.
    d) connective tissue.

11. John's wife comes in to visit John almost daily. John's wife always seems upset and tearful when they leave. Today you have an opportunity to sit and get to know them better. This can

    a) improve customer satisfaction.
    b) decrease their stress.
    c) increase their quality of life.
    d) do all of the above.

12. One function of the kidneys is to

    a) help regulate blood pressure.
    b) collect urine.
    c) release corticosteroids.
    d) support body metabolism.

13. Self-confidence and cooperation with others typically develop when a person is

    a) 4–5 years old.
    b) 6–11 years old.
    c) 12–19 years old.
    d) 20–34 years old.

14. You can reduce your risk of developing dementia by

    a) not using aluminum pots and pans when cooking.
    b) eating healthy foods and exercising.
    c) avoiding artificial sweeteners.
    d) avoiding aluminum-based deodorants.

15. Osteoarthritis most often affects the joints of the

    a) hips, lower back, and knees.
    b) fingers and toes.
    c) shoulders and neck.
    d) arms and hands.

16. An example of a modifiable risk factor would be

    a) old age.
    b) being female.
    c) alcohol use.
    d) ethnic background.

17. Understanding disease processes helps the nursing assistant to

    a) understand the importance of delegated tasks.
    b) care for the resident in a holistic manner.
    c) identify and diagnose abnormal conditions.
    d) both a and b.

18. Theresa is a 78-year-old resident with Alzheimer's. They are often restless and anxious, especially in the evenings. You can help reduce Theresa's anxiety by

    a) looking at a photo album together.
    b) giving them some clean towels to fold.
    c) turning on the TV for them.
    d) both a and b.

19. Plaques and tangles in the brain are characteristic of

    a) Lewy body dementia.
    b) vascular dementia.
    c) Alzheimer's disease.
    d) Parkinson's disease.

20. Anna is a resident who is in the early stages of dementia. They are on medication for Alzheimer's disease. This medication can help Anna by

    a) reversing the effects of Alzheimer's.
    b) delaying the progression of dementia.
    c) stopping the disease from progressing.
    d) providing a cure for Alzheimer's.

21. Modifiable risk factors include all of the following EXCEPT

    a) high blood pressure.
    b) alcoholism.
    c) genetics.
    d) depression.

22. An example of a chronic skin disorder would be

    a) pressure injuries.
    b) psoriasis.
    c) shingles.
    d) varicella.

23. A resident who is diagnosed with leukemia has cancer of the

    a) adrenal glands.
    b) bone marrow.
    c) immune system.
    d) brain and spinal column.

24. One of the first symptoms of dementia is

    a) not recognizing close relatives.
    b) difficulty swallowing foods.
    c) short-term memory loss.
    d) sexual inappropriateness.

25. Estelle is an elderly resident with dementia. This afternoon you find them by the nurse's desk pacing back and forth, visibly upset. The first thing you should do for Estelle is to

    a) assist them to the bathroom and ensure that they are dry and comfortable.
    b) encourage them to visit another resident in the facility.
    c) give them an art project to work on in their room.
    d) tell the nurse that Estelle needs medication for anxiety.

26. Treatment for type 2 diabetes often begins with

    a) oral medications.
    b) insulin injections.
    c) a balanced diet.
    d) eliminating desserts.

27. Doreen is a resident with moderate dementia. At supper, you notice that they have had a large, loose incontinent stool. When you attempt to toilet and change Doreen, they become upset and start yelling at you. You should

    a) continue attempting to toilet and clean Doreen.
    b) let them rest for a few minutes and then reapproach them.
    c) wait until they are ready to go to bed to clean them.
    d) tell Doreen that they have to be washed or their skin will break down.

28. A diagnosis of Alzheimer's disease is confirmed by

a) extensive laboratory tests.
b) autopsy after the resident's death.
c) the resident's signs and symptoms.
d) mental examination by the doctor.

29. A masklike facial appearance, difficulty swallowing, tremors, and an inability to move purposely are symptoms of

a) myocardial infarction.
b) Parkinson's disease.
c) Alzheimer's disease.
d) epilepsy.

30. Offering smoothies to a resident who is receiving chemotherapy may help with

a) mouth sores.
b) bone pain.
c) diarrhea.
d) alopecia.

31. Cancer that has metastasized to other areas of the body is identified as

a) stage I.
b) stage II.
c) stage III.
d) stage IV.

32. Most cancers are caused by

a) genetic makeup.
b) infections.
c) lifestyle choices.
d) environmental factors.

33. When cancer spreads or moves to other areas of the body, it is called

a) metastasis.
b) a benign tumor.
c) a carcinogen.
d) stage I cancer.

34. You work in a long-term care facility that has a unit designed for residents with dementia. Today you have noticed that one of your coworkers has been very impatient and short-tempered with their residents. You should

a) tell your coworker that you will cover for them while they take their cigarette break.
b) ignore it; all caregivers have difficult days.
c) report your observations to the nurse right away.
d) suggest to the coworker that they take some time off from work.

35. Lydia is a 42-year-old woman who has been diagnosed with stage II breast cancer. They tell you that they are trying a new herbal supplement to help fight the cancer. You should

a) ask Lydia which herbal supplement they are taking and then update the nurse.
b) tell them that herbal supplements are not effective against cancer.
c) search the Internet for information on the supplement to give Lydia.
d) ask Lydia to wait until after their cancer treatments to start a supplement.

36. Palliative care is designed to help those residents who

a) are expected to live 3 months or less.
b) have decided to stop treatments to cure their cancer.
c) have a terminal disease and wish comfort measures only.
d) need relief from the symptoms and stress of their cancer.

37. You are caring for a resident with dementia who often refuses to have their incontinence garment changed. The most effective phrase to use when assisting them to the bathroom is

a) "Let's go to the toilet."
b) "It's time to change your brief."
c) "Let's just freshen up a bit."
d) "I'm going to take you to the bathroom now."

38. Christian is a 38-year-old man with stage III lung cancer. This means that the cancer

    a) is a larger tumor but is confined to the lungs.
    b) has started to spread into the tissues surrounding the lungs.
    c) has spread to other areas of the body and lymph nodes.
    d) is a slow-growing tumor.

39. Almost half of all cancers are caused by

    a) unprotected sun exposure.
    b) hepatitis B and C.
    c) exposure to asbestos.
    d) tobacco smoke.

40. One of your residents with dementia has been very wakeful throughout the night. They have attempted to get out of bed unassisted several times. To help them sleep better at night, you should

    a) keep the unit as quiet and calm as possible.
    b) move them to a room next to the nurse's station.
    c) keep the awake until at least 10:00 p.m.
    d) ask the nurse if they can give the resident a sleeping pill.

41. Chemotherapy is a treatment option that consists of

    a) surgical removal of the tumor and surrounding tissue.
    b) a beam of radiation aimed directly at the cancer.
    c) administering medications via IV, injection, or pills.
    d) targeting a specific area only.

42. Alberto is a resident with late-stage Alzheimer's. They are no longer able to speak or follow directives. An appropriate activity for Alberto would be

    a) bingo.
    b) arts and crafts.
    c) morning exercise group.
    d) an ice-cream social.

13.E Choose the best response to the following scenarios.

1. Two residents who both have dementia are fighting in the hallway. What should you do?

    a) Get their attention by yelling "Stop" and then separate them.
    b) Talk in a soft tone while separating them.
    c) Explain resident rights to both residents.
    d) Keep calm and call 911.

2. You are caring for Alicia, a 32-year-old woman with stage IV breast cancer. They have decided to stop treatments and return home to be with their husband and daughter. Alicia's mother asks you to speak with them and convince them to continue treatments. What should you do?

    a) Tell them you will speak with Alicia privately.
    b) Allow them to express their feelings and then update the nurse.
    c) Tell them to call the doctor for information on treatment options.
    d) Contact the social worker and ask them to speak with Alicia's family.

3. One of your residents has been battling leukemia for 3 years. Today they tell you that they want to die. What should you do?

   a) Allow them to talk about their feelings.
   b) Agree with them that 3 years is a long time to be ill.
   c) Tell them that this is not an appropriate thing to say.
   d) Tell them that it will get better.

4. You notice one of your residents with dementia crawling around on the floor of their room. What should you do?

   a) Ask the nurse to sedate the resident with medication.
   b) Nicely ask the resident to stop being so disruptive.
   c) Put the resident back in bed and tell them to remain there.
   d) Make sure the resident is safe and try to redirect them.

5. Your resident is 15 minutes late for bingo and is in a hurry to get up. What is the best response?

   a) Explain to the resident that it is important to move slowly when going from a sitting to a standing position.
   b) Tell the resident to hurry; bingo already started.
   c) Tell the resident that it would be better not to attend bingo today.
   d) Take the resident's place at the bingo table until they get there.

6. One of your residents has been diagnosed with breast cancer. They have been online looking for alternative cancer treatments and ask for your opinion. What should you do?

   a) Tell them that the decision for treatment options is very personal and that they should talk with their doctor.
   b) Explain to them that they must listen to the doctors' advice for treatment options.
   c) Offer an alternative healing website that one of your other residents used and was happy with.
   d) Tell them they should talk to the nurse about continuing with the treatment plan the doctor ordered.

7. You are caring for a 35-year-old who has cancer. Their doctor has recommended they have blood transfusions, but they have refused due to their beliefs. What should you do?

   a) Try and persuade them to take the treatment.
   b) Call in the social worker to talk with them and their family.
   c) Show them the latest statistics on blood transfusions.
   d) Respect their wishes and provide the care that they will accept.

8. A resident whom you are caring for has Alzheimer's. They tell you they are waiting for their husband to visit. You know that their husband has been dead for 20 years. What should you do?

   a) Tell them that you will let them know if you see their husband and redirect them to another activity.
   b) Tell them that their husband will not be coming to see them.
   c) Ask the nurse to give them some medicine to calm their nerves.
   d) Remind them that their husband passed away some time ago and then offer to take them to activities.

9. You are caring for a resident who has middle-stage Alzheimer's disease. You find them dressed in their best clothing. They tell you that they are going out to church, even though you know there are no services at the facility that day. What should you do?

   a) Offer to take them to church when you are done with your shift.
   b) Offer them a visit from the resident chaplain.
   c) Arrange a taxi for their ride and call the church so that they can be prepared for the resident.
   d) Tell them that they cannot go to church and change them into more appropriate clothing.

10. Clarence is a 78-year-old resident with lung disease. They ask you to take them to the designated smoking area. What is the best response?

    a) Tell them that you will update the nurse and then help them as instructed.
    b) Offer them a light.
    c) Tell them that they are sick and should not be smoking.
    d) Take their cigarettes and give the cigarettes to the nurse.

11. While you are bathing a resident with dementia, they starts to yell and scream. What should you do?

    a) Ignore their yelling since this is common with dementia.
    b) Proceed with the bath as quickly as possible.
    c) Do your best to stay calm and keep the resident safe.
    d) Leave them alone until they are calm.

12. You are caring for a resident with cancer who tells you that they are sick because the doctor gave them the wrong medicine. How should you respond?

    a) Agree with them; you know this doctor has made these types of mistakes before.
    b) Ask them what they mean by this and then update the nurse.
    c) Understand that it is probably just the medication making them say this.
    d) Politely listen to them while proceeding with your caregiving.

13. You are caring for a resident who has dementia. They take their pants off in the dining room during supper. What should you do?

    a) Remove the other residents from the area, then pull up their pants so they can resume eating.
    b) Ask the nurse if they can eat all their meals in their room.
    c) Help them pull up their pants and then assist them to the bathroom.
    d) After pulling up their pants, put a belt on them so that they cannot take off their pants by themself.

14. You are caring for Tim, they have a history of being aggressive. While you are bringing them their lunch they begin yelling and push the plate off the table. What should you do?

    a) Yell back at them and tell them they are not to yell at you
    b) Leave the room so as not to anger them further
    c) Remain calm and acknowledge their feelings
    d) Tell your supervisor you refuse to care for Tim after that interaction

Module 14: Rehabilitative Nursing

14.A Matching Definitions

_____ 1. Laryngectomy

_____ 2. Passive range of motion

_____ 3. ADLs

_____ 4. Dysarthria

_____ 5. IADLs

_____ 6. Apraxia

_____ 7. Active range of motion

A. Nervous system disorder in which a person is unable to perform a task when asked to do so

B. Activities of daily living, related to daily care

C. Exercises in which the nursing assistant is physically moving the resident's joint

D. Activities of daily life that require the use of instruments, tools, or appliances

E. Exercises in which the resident is actively participating and is moving the joint themself

F. Surgical removal of the larynx

G. Impaired muscular control, causing difficulty in forming words

14.B Reflective Short-Answer Exercises

Scenario 1:

Trudy is a resident recovering from a recent stroke. They are in the facility trying to regain strength and the function of their right side. You need to assist them with walking to the dining room. They become angry when you put the gait belt around their waist; they don't like it. While you are helping them walk, they become weak and almost fall. You sit them back down in the wheelchair and wheel them into the dining room.

1. What benefits would Trudy gain by ambulating to the dining room for each meal?

_____

_____

_____

_____

2. What level of assistance do you think Trudy might need with ambulation?

_____

_____

_____

_____

3. Trudy's care plan states they are to ambulate with an assist of one. Can you get more help and use two nursing assistants to walk them to the dining room?

_____

_____

_____

_____

4. What safety interventions must you consider before ambulating Trudy?

_____

_____

_____

_____

5. What assistive devices might help to steady Trudy during ambulation?

_____

_____

_____

_____

6. What else besides ambulation could help Trudy prevent a contracture from their stroke?

_____

_____

_____

_____

Scenario 2:

Izetta is a 65-year-old woman who recently suffered a stroke. They now have right-sided weakness and partial blindness in their right eye. They are admitted to a long-term care facility for physical and occupational therapy. Izetta will need assistance with tasks, including grooming.

1. How could you help Izetta but still preserve their self-esteem?

_____

_____

_____

_____

2. How would you put on Izetta's shirt, given their right-sided weakness?

_____

_____

_____

_____

3. What should you do before helping them put their glasses on?

_____

_____

_____

_____

4. Now that Izetta has partial blindness, they will need to wear glasses throughout the day. What could you do to help them adjust?

_____

_____

_____

_____

Scenario 3:

Harlan is a 67-year-old man who was in a motor vehicle accident four weeks ago. They suffered a fractured leg. Their right hand was crushed and required surgery. Harlan has been transferred to a rehabilitation unit to recover from the accident and regain their strength. Their goal is to return home to live independently.

1. Do you think Harlan would benefit from physical therapy? If so, how?

    _____
    _____
    _____
    _____

2. For which injuries might they benefit from physical therapy?

    _____
    _____
    _____
    _____

3. Do you think Harlan would benefit from occupational therapy? If so, how?

    _____
    _____
    _____
    _____

4. For which injuries might they benefit from occupational therapy?

    _____
    _____
    _____
    _____

5. After Harlan is discharged from therapy services, what could the nursing assistant do to help them maintain their ability level?

    _____
    _____
    _____
    _____

14.C   Fill in the blanks using terms found in the word bank.

ligament   digestive system   active

disabilities   physical therapist   maximize

financial   fall   family members

occupational therapist

1. The _____ is responsible for evaluating residents with a variety of disorders and is geared toward improving fine motor skills such as handling and manipulating small objects, like keys, dials, and buttons.

2. Occupational therapy services always involve the resident. They may also involve _____ and caretakers.

3. Most injuries that occur to people over the age of 65 result from a _____.

4. _____ range-of-motion exercises are when the resident is able to participate in the exercises with little or no help from the nursing assistant.

5. Walking and other types of movement help the motility in the _____ to prevent constipation.

6. The goal of therapy services is to restore prior ability or to _____ potential.

7. A contracture is the physical shortening of a _____ or muscle.

8. The _____ initially evaluates the resident for meeting rehabilitation needs and works with the resident in improving large, gross motor skills.

9. Injuries resulting from a fall may cause _____ strain.

10. Hot and cold applications can be dangerous for residents with cognitive _____.

14.D   Multiple-Choice Exercises

1. Moving an arm or leg away from the midline of the body is called

    a) flexion.
    b) abduction.
    c) dorsiflexion.
    d) adduction.

2. You notice your resident having difficulty swallowing and update the nurse. The MOST likely next step is that the

    a) speech therapist will assess the resident.
    b) physical therapist will provide the resident with adaptive tools.
    c) occupational therapist will assess the resident.
    d) nurse must feed the resident during meals.

3. A resident who has just received a prosthetic hand would MOST likely need

    a) speech therapy.
    b) a restorative aide.
    c) occupational therapy.
    d) activities therapy.

4. Expressive aphasia is a disorder commonly treated by a(n)

    a) occupational therapist.
    b) physical therapist.
    c) surgeon.
    d) speech therapist.

5. Claire is a long-term care resident who needs to be ambulated twice a day. The person responsible for this would be the

   a) nursing assistant.
   b) charge nurse.
   c) activities director.
   d) occupational therapist.

6. Dwayne is a resident who has recently had a hip replacement and should not bend forward at the hip. An adaptive device that might help them be more independent when dressing is

   a) a button aid.
   b) a toilet seat riser.
   c) a sock aid.
   d) elastic shoelaces.

7. Assisting a resident with ambulation helps

   a) reduce swelling in the legs.
   b) prevent contractures.
   c) maintain muscle tone.
   d) do all of the above.

8. You are performing passive range-of-motion exercises on Agatha's knee. They wince in pain with the movement. You should

   a) stop the exercises and inform the nurse that Agatha is having pain.
   b) let Agatha rest for five minutes and then try again.
   c) continue with the exercises to help loosen the muscles.
   d) skip range-of-motion exercises for the day.

9. You can assist the resident who is independent with ambulation by

   a) telling them they must walk to the dining room for meals.
   b) encouraging them to attend group activities offered that day.
   c) removing their wheelchair from their room.
   d) remaining close to them when they walk.

10. Juan's care plan states that they ambulate with an assist of one. This means you will need to

    a) use a gait belt with at least one hand on it at all times.
    b) ask another nursing assistant to help you.
    c) give them verbal reminders to walk each day.
    d) use a gait belt only if they are feeling weak or unsteady.

11. The nurse asks you to apply an ice pack to a resident's knee to reduce swelling and pain. The application should be kept on the area no longer than

    a) 3–5 minutes.
    b) 10–15 minutes.
    c) 20–30 minutes.
    d) 60 minutes.

12. You notice that Christian has recently needed more assistance with tasks like brushing their teeth and shaving. You should

    a) alert the nurse and continue to encourage independence.
    b) update the physical and occupational therapists.
    c) do nothing; this is a normal part of aging.
    d) shave and brush their teeth for them so they don't become frustrated.

13. Decreasing the angle of the joint is called

    a) adduction.
    b) hyperextension.
    c) flexion.
    d) rotation.

14. A fall in an older resident may lead to

    a) increase in level of care.
    b) immobility.
    c) depression.
    d) all of the above.

15. Range-of-motion exercises are performed to

    a) prevent contractures.
    b) strengthen a weak arm or leg after an injury.
    c) rehabilitate a paralyzed arm or leg after a stroke.
    d) do all of the above.

16. Before you assist a resident with ambulation, they must be wearing

    a) shoes or have bare feet.
    b) socks or bathroom slippers.
    c) footwear with a nonskid sole.
    d) what they find most comfortable.

17. Encouraging your resident to perform tasks such as washing the face helps to

    a) maintain muscle mass.
    b) provide range-of-motion exercise.
    c) maintain self-esteem.
    d) do all of the above.

14.E Choose the best response to the following scenarios.

1. Your resident has asked you to help them to the toilet. While you are trying to put your gait belt around the resident for this transfer, they say, "I need to go now," and then try to stand up alone. What should you do?

    a) Let them stand up and ambulate without the gait belt.
    b) Stand in front of them while applying the gait belt and remind them of safety.
    c) Refuse to help them because they are being unreasonable.
    d) Leave them in the restroom and get the supervisor.

2. You are caring for a resident who has been sitting in their wheelchair for the past 2 hours. They are now anxious and begin to stand unassisted. What should you do?

    a) Assist them to ambulate if not contraindicated.
    b) Put them in a reclining chair in the facility's lounge.
    c) Help them back to the bed so they may rest.
    d) Place them in front of the television.

3. You are assigned to ambulate a resident who requires an assist of one and a walker. They tell you that they do not want the gait belt on them, since they are using the walker. What should you do?

    a) Respect your resident's wishes and do not use the gait belt.
    b) Ambulate the resident with an assist of two and no gait belt.
    c) Reinforce to the resident the importance of using the gait belt and report to the supervisor.
    d) Tell the nurse that the resident doesn't need the gait belt.

4. Your resident is doing well and seems to be able to transfer with an assist of two instead of the mechanical lift as the care plan states. What should you do?

    a) Transfer the resident with an assist of two so they continue to improve.
    b) Use the mechanical lift and report your findings to the supervisor.
    c) Transfer the resident with an assist of two and a gait belt for added safety.
    d) Ask your coworkers how they transferred the resident.

5. Your resident is placed on bed rest following surgery but insists they can walk to the bathroom with your assistance. What should you do?

   a) Help the resident to the restroom; it is best to keep them moving.
   b) Get another nursing assistant to assist you in case they are not strong enough.
   c) Reinforce to the resident the importance of remaining on bed rest and offer the bedpan.
   d) Ask the nurse to assist the resident to the bathroom.

6. Your resident is self-conscious regarding their prosthetic eye and asks for privacy while placing it. What should you do?

   a) Pull the privacy curtain, make sure they have the call light, and leave the room.
   b) Leave the room but keep the door open in case they need help.
   c) Reassure them that you have seen this before and can do it for them.
   d) None of the above; they should not do this themself.

This page intentionally left blank.

Module 15: Observation and Charting

15.A   Matching Definitions

_____ 1. Oral reporting

_____ 2. Data

_____ 3. Medical error

_____ 4. Medical abbreviation

_____ 5. Subjective data

_____ 6. Objective data

_____ 7. Electronic health record

_____ 8. Incident report

A. Relaying information verbally to another member of the healthcare team

B. Information that cannot be measured; a feeling or opinion

C. The digital version of a resident's paper chart

D. A document that is filled out to describe a specific occurrence of exposure or accident that led to, or had the potential to lead to, an injury

E. Information that can be measured; tangible and concrete

F. Pieces of information

G. A mistake made by a member of the healthcare team before or during caregiving

H. A shortened medical word or group of words

15.B   Reflective Short-Answer Exercises

Margaret is caring for Mrs. Lee, who is on a strict NPO diet. Mrs. Lee calls Margaret to their room complaining of dry mouth. Margaret offers them a small cup of ice chips, and 30 minutes later Mrs. Lee has vomited twice, holding their stomach, and is complaining of stomach pain. Margaret obtains the resident's vital signs and then reports to the nurse.

1. NPO stands for "nothing by mouth." Based on this, what did Margaret do wrong?

_____

_____

_____

_____

2. How did the medical error happen in this scenario?

_____

_____

_____

_____

3. Could the medical error have been prevented? If so, how?

_____

_____

_____

_____

4. Should Margaret have asked the nurse to clarify the meaning of NPO? Is there another way for them to check the meaning of NPO?

_____
_____
_____
_____

5. What should Margaret have told the nurse before offering the ice chips to Mrs. Lee?

_____
_____
_____
_____

6. What is the objective data that Margaret should report to the nurse?

_____
_____
_____
_____

7. Should Margaret report the objective data to the nurse right away or chart it at the end of their work shift? Why should they report the data at that time?

_____
_____
_____
_____

8. What is the subjective data in this scenario?

_____
_____
_____
_____

15.C Fill in the blanks using terms found in the word bank.

oral report	lives	subjective data
care plan	documented	confidentiality
computer	provided	incident report
medical abbreviations	objective data	paper
eliminate		

1. It is important to maintain _____ during and after the documentation process.

2. Many medical errors occur because of the use of _____.

3. The _____ is a tool created by the nurse to communicate what the nursing assistant needs to do to safely care for a resident.

4. A resident's urinary output for an 8-hour shift is an example of _____.

5. The general rule in healthcare is "If it is not _____, it is not done."

6. A(n) _____ is given to your supervisor or another member of the healthcare team usually at the end of the shift.

7. Mistakes in healthcare can cost _____.

8. Healthcare professionals are trying to _____ the use of medical abbreviations.

9. Documentation can be done on _____ or on a _____, according to facility policy.

10. Thinking that a resident is feeling ill is an example of _____.

11. It is the responsibility of the nursing assistant to document only the care that they have _____.

12. The _____ is a form that is supplied by the facility for documentation of an accident or exposure.

15.D Multiple-Choice Exercises

1. Using fewer medical abbreviations means that

    a) nurses use fewer abbreviations in their oral reports.
    b) abbreviations aren't used when doctors write orders.
    c) there is a decrease in healthcare errors.
    d) medical errors are eliminated.

2. The nurse informs you that Mrs. Jones needs to have their HS snack. You are unsure what time you should be giving the snack. You should

    a) ask one of the other nursing assistants.
    b) look it up in the dictionary.
    c) ask the nurse for clarification.
    d) give the snack as soon as it comes from the kitchen.

3. Documentation completed by the nursing assistant may include

    a) flow sheets.
    b) tracking forms.
    c) the resident's medical chart.
    d) both a and b.

4. While giving a resident their scheduled shower, you notice that they have a reddened area on their back. You should

    a) report this to the nurse when you have completed the shower.
    b) report this to the nurse at the end of your shift.
    c) leave a note for the nurse at their desk.
    d) inform the resident's family.

5. When you attempted to feed Mrs. Johnson their lunch, they became very upset and said, "I don't want any of this! I want to lie down! Leave me alone!" When reporting this, you tell the nurse that Mrs. Johnson

    a) doesn't have an appetite.
    b) was too tired to eat.
    c) was angry and uncooperative.
    d) was upset and refused their meal.

6. You think Mr. Thao has a sore throat because they are refusing to eat their breakfast. This is an example of

    a) objective data.
    b) subjective data.
    c) therapeutic communication.
    d) evidence-based information.

7. When discovering new information that is out of the normal range for a resident, you should give an oral report to

   a) the nurse at the end of your shift.
   b) the nurse right away.
   c) the caregiver relieving you.
   d) both b and c.

8. If the nursing assistant makes an error in the chart, they should

   a) write the word "error" and sign.
   b) draw a line through the error and initial.
   c) use erasable ink to keep the chart easier to read.
   d) get a new sheet of paper to reduce confusion.

9. Mr. Lopez ate 75% of their lunch and drank 240 cc of milk and 120 cc of coffee. The appropriate time to document this in the facility's meal sheets is

   a) at the end of your shift.
   b) as soon as they tell you they are full.
   c) before leaving on your afternoon break.
   d) when you have enough time.

10. An example of subjective data would be

    a) a fever of 101.2°F.
    b) thinking a resident has the flu.
    c) foul-smelling urine.
    d) a resident wincing when they move.

11. The term used to refer to the nearer of two points on the body is

    a) proximal.
    b) distal.
    c) medial.
    d) posterior.

12. You are charting at the end of your shift when you notice that a resident had turned on their call light. After assisting the resident, you forget to go back to the nurse's desk where you had been charting. You should

    a) call and leave an oral report for the nurse.
    b) promptly return to the facility and complete your assigned charting.
    c) ask one of your coworkers to complete the charting.
    d) finish the charting when you return to the facility for your next shift.

15.E   Choose the best response to the following scenarios.

1. You are assisting a resident with dementia in the shower. They suddenly become very upset and bite you on your arm. The skin isn't broken, and the area doesn't hurt. What is the appropriate action to take?

   a) Do nothing since there doesn't seem to be any damage to your skin.
   b) Report the incident to the nurse at the end of your shift.
   c) Wash out the wound and continue with the resident's shower.
   d) Ensure that your resident is safe, report to the nurse, and complete an incident report.

2. You enter a resident's room and find them grimacing, slouched over, and holding their stomach. The best response is to

   a) assume they need to use the restroom.
   b) ask them if they are okay and be prepared to assist if needed.
   c) tell the nurse they are in pain and await further directives from the nurse.
   d) come back later when they are feeling better.

3. You make a mistake while charting. The appropriate action to take is to

   a) erase the mistake the best you can.
   b) use correctional fluid to cover the mistake.
   c) draw a single line through the mistake and initial.
   d) ask the supervisor to correct the document for you.

4. You discover skin tears and bruises on one of your home health residents. You should

    a) call the resident's son and update them on the injuries.

    b) ask the resident what happened, update the nurse supervisor, and then document the injuries.

    c) dial 911 and ask for directives.

    d) treat the injuries and then call 911.

This page intentionally left blank.

Module 16: Death and Dying

16.A Definitions

Write a definition for the following terms.

1. Cheyne-Stokes breathing: _____

2. Mottling: _____

16.B Reflective Short-Answer Exercises

Darshan is an older resident who is dying of prostate cancer. They are a practicing Hindu and have pictures of Hindu gods on their bedside table. Darshan's family has been chanting at their bedside for the last 2 days. Today they are in a coma. They have not voided for the last 24 hours. They have not had a bowel movement for the last 5 days. Darshan can no longer take anything in by mouth. You notice that they have now started Cheyne-Stokes breathing, and their lower legs are purple in color.

1. How would you perform your job with Darshan's family present around the clock?

    _____

    _____

    _____

    _____

2. What respiratory changes tell you Darshan is close to death? How could you explain this to the family?

    _____

    _____

    _____

    _____

3. Do you think Darshan can hear the chanting? Why or why not?

    _____

    _____

    _____

    _____

4. How could the chanting provide Darshan comfort?

    _____

    _____

    _____

    _____

5. Is it normal that Darshan has not had a bowel movement for 5 days? Why or why not?

    _____

    _____

    _____

    _____

6. Is it normal that Darshan has not voided for a whole day? Why or why not?

_____

_____

_____

_____

7. How can you help Darshan stay comfortable now that they are exhibiting the Cheyne-Stokes breathing pattern?

_____

_____

_____

_____

8. Should you accommodate the family's round-the-clock vigil in Darshan's room?

_____

_____

_____

_____

9. What feelings might Darshan's family members be experiencing?

_____

_____

_____

_____

16.C   Fill in the blanks using terms found in the word bank.

decrease	apnea	terminal
doctor	mottling	death
oral care	dignity	religion
honored	cardiovascular	physical

1. _____ is the appearance of purplish marbling on the skin as a result of poor blood flow to the extremities.

2. Rights of the dying patient include having an advance directive, being able to make their own choices regarding care, and being treated with _____.

3. People who die from chronic conditions may go through a series of _____ changes such as mottling, dusky nail beds, and respiratory changes.

4. _____ is a part of life.

5. The nursing assistant should provide _____ each time the resident is repositioned.

6. As the dying process continues, the _____ system slows down, often resulting in an irregular heartbeat and low blood pressure.

7. As the body begins to slow, appetite and thirst _____; it can frighten family members when the resident stops eating and drinking.

8. You cannot assume that everyone is the same _____ or has the same beliefs as you do.

9. You should feel _____ to help your resident and their loved ones through the life event of passing away.

10. Hospice services are available to the resident if the diagnosis is _____ and death is expected within the next six months.

11. Cheyne-Stokes breathing is a pattern of fast, shallow breathing followed by slow, deep breathing, with periods of _____.

12. The _____ pronounces the resident deceased.

16.D Multiple-Choice Exercises

1. Thao is a 30-year-old resident who is dying of cancer. Their family has been by their bedside for the last 3 days. Thao's mother takes you aside and explains that they wish the family to clean and dress Thao in their burial clothes after they die. You should

   a) report this to the nurse to get further directives.
   b) tell Thao's mother that only staff can provide post-mortem care.
   c) ask why Thao's mother wishes the family to do Thao's care.
   d) contact a representative of the family's faith.

2. The goal of hospice service is

   a) recovery from a terminal illness.
   b) managing symptoms and increasing quality of life.
   c) managing medications that increase survival.
   d) providing long-term support for chronic illness.

3. Edwin is an 86-year-old resident who is dying of heart failure. Their daughter is at their bedside. Their daughter tells you that Edwin's breathing will stop for a minute before starting again. The daughter is clearly upset by this. You should

   a) tell them that you will start oxygen for Edwin.
   b) immediately report this to the nurse, as it is abnormal.
   c) reassure them that apnea is a normal part of the dying process.
   d) ask them to step out of the room.

4. When caring for a resident who is dying, you should

   a) reposition the resident every 2 hours.
   b) reposition the resident every hour.
   c) provide oral care every 2–3 hours.
   d) use large comforters and blankets.

5. Wanda is a 62-year-old who is dying of cancer. When you enter Wanda's room, you notice that they makes a gurgling noise when they breathe. You should

   a) reposition Wanda and raise the head of the bed.
   b) do a finger-sweep and Heimlich maneuver.
   c) ask the nurse to suction Wanda's airways.
   d) start Wanda on oxygen for their comfort.

6. Hospice services can be delivered at

   a) a resident's home.
   b) a nursing home.
   c) a hospital.
   d) all of the above.

7. The last sense to fade during the dying process is

   a) touch.
   b) taste.
   c) smell.
   d) hearing.

8. Cheyne-Stokes breathing is characterized by

   a) long, deep breaths through the nose and out the nose.
   b) fast, shallow breathing followed by slow, deep breathing.
   c) a gurgling noise caused by saliva in the throat.
   d) a rattling sound coming from the chest.

9. Cora is dying of emphysema. They have oxygen on at 2L per minute via nasal cannula. Their son tells you that Cora has been trying to take their oxygen off. Cora says they don't want to wear it anymore, but their son is insisting that they keep the oxygen on. You should

   a) tell Cora that they need to keep their oxygen on.
   b) tell their son that this is a normal part of the dying process.
   c) put their oxygen back on using an oxygen mask.
   d) update the nurse and wait for directives.

10. The first stage of grief is typically

    a) bargaining.
    b) denial.
    c) depression.
    d) anger.

11. When providing post-mortem care, the nursing assistant is responsible for all of the following EXCEPT

    a) bathing the resident's body.
    b) putting the resident's dentures in.
    c) listening for a heartbeat.
    d) tidying the resident's room.

16.E   Choose the best response to the following scenarios.

1. Bertha's family has been at their bedside for the last 5 days. As you approach Bertha's room, you hear loud angry voices. You discover two of Bertha's daughters arguing with each other. What should you do?

   a) Remain outside the room to allow them privacy.
   b) Politely intervene and encourage them to go for a walk.
   c) Report the incident to the facility's social worker.
   d) Tell them that their arguing will just upset their mother.

2. You are taking care of a resident who is dying. They tell you that they are seeing beautiful butterflies and angels in the room. What should you do?

   a) Tell them that they are having a hallucination and that it is a normal part of dying.
   b) Leave the resident alone and then report this to the family.
   c) Ask the resident to explain what they are seeing.
   d) Turn on the television while you are caregiving to distract them.

3. Your dying resident asks you to say the Lord's Prayer with them, but you don't know it. What should you do?

   a) Offer to hold the resident's hand while they say the prayer.
   b) Explain to the resident that you are not Catholic.
   c) Search for the prayer on your cell phone and then pray with them.
   d) Ask the resident to wait until the priest arrives.

4. The family is in the room of a resident you are caring for. The resident is dying and the family members are talking about them like they have already passed away. What should you do?

   a) Tell the family that they are being rude.
   b) Set a good example by speaking to the resident while caring for them.
   c) Read the family the dying resident's bill of rights.
   d) Turn up the television so that the resident can't hear this.

5. Your resident passed away last night. The family calls to say they would like to pack up their loved one's personal belongings. What should you do?

   a) Try to avoid them so you don't make them upset.
   b) Have the belongings packed for them and waiting at the nurse's desk.
   c) Pack up the belongings with the family members, reminding them that they will feel better soon.
   d) Tell them that you are sorry for their loss and then allow them to pack their loved one's belongings.

6. Your resident has died and it is your responsibility to perform post-mortem care. You have never done this and are nervous. What should you do?

   a) Ask for assistance from another nursing assistant and remain professional.
   b) Refuse to care for the resident because it makes you uncomfortable.
   c) Care for the resident based on what you remember from your class.
   d) Inform the nurse that this is not in your scope of practice.

This page intentionally left blank.

Name _____

Module 17: Abuse

17.A Matching Definitions

No definitions listed in this module.

17.B Reflective Short-Answer Exercises

Julia is supposed to be transferred with a mechanical lift by two nursing assistants. The nursing assistant caring for Julia chose to transfer Julia by herself rather than wait for a coworker to help them. Julia fell during this transfer. They suffered head trauma and a broken hip and were transferred to the hospital.

1. In the story of Julia, what information is protected by HIPAA?

_____

_____

_____

_____

2. If the nursing assistant would have explained the risks of being transferred by one and not two assistants, and Julia agreed to a one assist, would this have followed informed consent standards? Why or why not?

_____

_____

_____

_____

3. What did the nursing assistant do when they chose to transfer Julia by themself rather than following the two-person assist as the care plan indicated?

_____

_____

_____

_____

4. Was the action in the story abuse? Why or why not?

_____

_____

_____

_____

5. What do you think will happen to the nursing assistant regarding their certification as a CNA?

_____

_____

_____

_____

17.C   Fill in the blanks using terms from the word bank.

mandatory reporter	abandonment	ombudsman
six hours	accountability	caregiver strain
behavior	HIPAA	treatment
identifiable	informed consent	investigations
ethics		

1. As a nursing assistant, you are considered a _____.

2. Leaving a resident alone and at risk for harm is considered _____.

3. A volunteer who advocates for the residents in a facility is a(n) _____.

4. The right to know what treatment options are available is _____.

5. HIPAA is a law that protects individually _____ health information.

6. Responsibility is having _____ for one's own actions.

7. _____ are beliefs or laws that provide freedom to act in certain ways.

8. Not logging off a computer after documenting care provided can be a violation of _____ laws.

9. Ethics are principles of right and wrong that drive our _____.

10. The resident has a right to refuse any _____ or action.

11. The Health and Safety Codes for California require nursing assistant training to include a minimum of _____ of instruction on preventing, recognizing, and reporting resident abuse.

12. Treating residents poorly can be a result of _____.

13. The California Department of Public Health is a state agency that completes surveys and _____.

17.D   Multiple-Choice Exercises

1. Mr. Thompson's care plan states that they transfer with two nursing assistants helping them. You notice that they are much stronger than when they were admitted to the facility. You think they could transfer with only one person assisting. Your FIRST step is to

    a) tell their family that Mr. Thompson can now be transferred with one person.
    b) change their care plan since they have improved.
    c) orally report their improvement to the nurse.
    d) update their medical care plan.

2. A document listing patient rights and responsibilities is often given to the resident

    a) upon discharge from the facility.
    b) only when there is a conflict between the resident and the facility.
    c) upon admission to the facility.
    d) only upon request.

3. You suspect that one of the other nursing assistants has been verbally abusive to one of your older residents. The best response would be to

   a) confront your coworker.
   b) report your suspicions to your supervisor.
   c) find out if your suspicions are right and then report.
   d) tell the resident's family so they can keep the resident safe.

4. Using a resident's phone without their knowledge is an example of

   a) misappropriation of funds.
   b) caregiver strain.
   c) negligence.
   d) invasion of privacy.

5. You enter a resident's room and see another nursing assistant slap the resident across the arm. You did not report it, since it only happened once. The person(s) who might be found guilty of abuse would be

   a) your coworker.
   b) the nurse for failing to supervise.
   c) you.
   d) both a and c.

6. The ombudsman is a volunteer who helps support resident rights by

   a) relaying residents' concerns to regulating bodies.
   b) teaching residents and their families about resident rights.
   c) promoting resident council meetings.
   d) doing all of the above.

7. Jane is an older resident who is unable to move on their own. Their care plan states that they are to be repositioned every 2 hours. You have been especially busy, and you decide that you are only able to reposition them every 4 hours. Because of this, Jane develops a pressure injury on their tailbone. This is an example of

   a) physical abuse.
   b) battery.
   c) neglect.
   d) both a and c.

8. The Health Insurance Portability and Accountability Act (HIPAA) protects a resident's right to

   a) keep their health information private.
   b) access their health records.
   c) make informed choices.
   d) control their finances.

17.E Choose the best response to the following scenarios.

1. One of the male residents at your work makes sexual comments to you while you are caring for them. The comments make you feel very uncomfortable. What should you do?

   a) Tell the resident that their behavior is not acceptable and report to your supervisor.
   b) Tell the resident's wife and request that the wife speak to the resident on your behalf.
   c) Ignore the resident's comments.
   d) Trade assignments with your coworker to avoid the resident.

2. The wife of one of your residents asks you for a copy of the resident's medical record. How should you respond?

   a) Make copies of the record for the wife since they are married.
   b) Do not make copies of the record, but allow the wife to read the resident's medical chart.
   c) Tell the wife that you are unable to make copies but will inform the nurse of their request.
   d) Ask the wife why they need this information.

3. While caring for one of your residents, you notice the care plan is not correct or updated. What should you do?

    a) Pencil in the correct information.
    b) Let your supervisor know that the care plan must be updated.
    c) Report your observations to your supervisor.
    d) Report your observations to the doctor.

4. A resident you care for on a regular basis says they appreciate the help you have provided. To thank you, they offer you $10 and say that you should "treat yourself." How should you respond?

    a) Thank the resident and tell them that you cannot accept tips.
    b) Keep the money to avoid hurting their feelings.
    c) Split the $10 among your coworkers.
    d) Tell the resident they are not allowed to keep cash in their room.

5. You witness a coworker verbally abuse a resident. The resident appears to ignore the comments, but later you find them crying. What is the best response?

    a) Tell the coworker that their conduct is unacceptable.
    b) Ignore the situation since there was no physical contact.
    c) Apologize to the resident for your coworker's rude behavior.
    d) Make sure the resident is safe and report the abuse immediately.